D1064638

Behavior of industrial work groups

Behavior of industrial work groups

Prediction and control

LEONARD R. SAYLES

Associate Professor

Graduate School of Business

Columbia University

NEW YORK · JOHN WILEY & SONS, INC.

London · Chapman & Hall, Limited

Library of Congress Catalog Card Number: 58—13468

Printed in the United States of America

For my mother

Preface

The pioneering Western Electric Studies provided a picture of the informal work group in industry that has persisted almost without change for a score of years. Many of our theories about and recommendations for practice in management carry with them implicit or explicit assumptions concerning the fixed characteristics of these groups.

This study has the conclusion that no such simple picture will suffice. In fact, the differences among work groups, in their attitudes and behavior within the industrial plant, may be of more significance to the student of industrial relations and the management and union administrators who must deal with plant level problems than their similarities. I am concerned here with portraying the whole array of informal group behavior; not only to present a realistic appraisal of human relations in industry, but also to provide some understanding why groups differ in their relations to management and the union, in their "morale" and productivity.

This is the first of what we hope will be a series of research studies at Columbia's Graduate School of Business on organizational behavior. In these studies we shall seek to break down the traditional boundaries that now separate what are essentially interrelated fields: formal organization and administration theory, human relations and personnel management, management decision making and production management, and collective bargaining. The basic objective of this work and the succeeding studies is to further our knowledge of the functioning of large-scale organizations embodying problems of the division of labor and extended hierarchies.

My descriptions and analysis are based on field investigations extending over several years, and I am indebted to the numerous companies and unions, their employees, and officials, who gave generously of their time and permitted an outsider to question, look, and listen, and frequently to intrude at will.

Professor William F. Whyte of Cornell and Dr. Eliot D. Chapple with patience and regularity offered me theoretical insight and confidence. Professor Margaret Chandler of the University of Illinois and Professor George Strauss of the University of Buffalo, as many footnotes reveal, supplied generous quantities of relevant case material. Professor James Kuhn, of our own faculty, who is conducting a challenging parallel inquiry, frequently supplied ideas and encouragement. The Bureau of Industrial Relations of the University of Michigan, through its Director, Professor John Riegel, was responsible for the financing of a large share of the field work and the attendant typing expenses. Dr. Riegel also read and criticized a first draft of the manuscript.

Columbia has provided both the stimulating environment and the physical facilities for the completion of this work. A researcher would be hard-pressed to find a university setting more suited to his needs.

Risha Sayles shared many of the tasks associated with the preparation of this volume.

LEONARD SAYLES

New York, New York
April 1, 1958

Contents

chapter 1

Commonplace observations; complex problems

The natural scientists learned long ago that everyday observations, although they are commonplace and universally experienced, are nonetheless of substantial importance. The falling of displaced objects, the occurrence of lightning, the changes in the structure of the tadpole, and an infinite number of other natural occurrences provoked investigation and thought which led to scientific knowledge. Even with modern advances in laboratory methods and theoretical knowledge, important discoveries in the physical sciences are often the result of chance observation of natural phenomena. The simplicity of the observation frequently belies the true complexity of the subject to be explored.

Practitioners in the field of industrial relations, facing a firing line of day-to-day problems, also see things which are often accepted as part of the "obvious" but which in reality demand some explanation. This study, in fact, deals with some commonplace observations and the attempt of a research project to provide a useful explanation of "why things happen the way they do."

One observation provoking research was the conclusion drawn by many people in personnel work and labor relations, that certain departments or work groups are "always troublesome" whereas others are "generally cooperative." These people find certain parts of their organizations consistently above average in terms of some criterion of cooperation and others consistently below the plant average.

Such observations as these are not limited to management, of course. Union leaders also note that some parts of their plants are "able to handle their own problems, and, when necessary, back up their union officials," whereas other groups "are always trying to make trouble for somebody and can never be satisfied." Some occupational groups may be known throughout an entire industry for their highly characteristic behavior.

Interesting, too, is the fact that work groups identified by management or the union as being atypical in their behavior often remain so over a long period of time, even though during this period there are changes in their supervision and membership, turnover among leaders in the local union, and shifts in management policy.

We are not asserting that such factors are unimportant in shaping group behavior, that union and management policy, the whims and fancies of leaders on both sides, the skills of supervisors, and the idiosyncrasies of individual employees do not play a vital part in determining the character of plant-level industrial relations. Rather, "radical" unionists, "bullheaded supervisors," and "troublemaking" employees are only a part of the picture. There must be special reasons why some departments always appear to have more than their share of disruption, while other departments are oases of harmony.

Concern with the incidence of the extremes of work group behavior is the point of departure for this study. Why does one work group support and encourage and, in fact, stimulate a highly aggressive informal leadership, whereas in another work area the same personality type languishes in obscurity? Why does a management policy or union decision cause a flurry of excitement and tension in one department and gain acceptance without so much as a question in an adjacent group? It is in this area of group behavior that market forces, union traditions, and historical developments in the union-management relationships have their minimum impact.

In reviewing the literature in the field of personnel management, it would appear that inadequate consideration has been given to *both* parties in the supervisor-subordinate relationship. Most of our attention has been concentrated on the supervisor.

In the not very distant past management assumed, and with some correctness, that each work group under its supervisor was a team. As a team they were dedicated to the best interests of the enterprise. The easy assumptions about spontaneous teamwork and group efforts directed toward the goals of the firm have been shattered in this century. We have grown accustomed to reports on restriction of output, antimanagement activities of a wide variety, and internal bickerings, and strife. However, we may have gone too far in taking such matters for granted.

The work group itself we have learned is the primary focus for registering discontent as well as the organizational mechanism for releasing productivity.[1] It is not the isolated individual workman, as many are prone to believe. Further, these groups are themselves the product of management decisions. In the succeeding chapters it will be possible to show that the organization and basic orientation of these groups follow the lines of work structure. The technology and organization of the plant are the architects of the work group, constructing with the materials of human interaction a variety of types of groups.

Thus, although changes in the leadership abilities of the supervisor may affect changes in the behavior of his work group, might it be that the characteristics of the work group limit severely the supervisor's range of behavior? More importantly, the temperament of the work group may be a significant determinant of what are appropriate or successful supervisory methods. This study, therefore, takes up the differing demands which work groups make on their supervisors, managements, and unions. These groups have evolved persistent, recurring modes of adjustment to their industrial environment.

Another objective of this study is to provide the tools of prediction for administrators who must deal with work groups in large organizations.

There are important values here. By being able to identify *in advance* the work groups that will support or attack management or union programs, the administrator gains a major tactical advantage. Given the knowledge of what kinds of situations produce certain behavior patterns in work groups, he can:

1. Become sensitive to these areas and, by concentrating leadership talent and attention, head off some of the complications. Forewarning is often more than half the victory.
2. Change the internal dynamics of the plant so that new and perhaps more satisfactory work group patterns are created.

In either case the administrator is likely to be coping with the industrial relations problems of his organization in a manner calculated to give longer lasting solutions than those achieved by the usual last-

[1] Cf. Edward A. Shils, "The Study of the Primary Group," *The Policy Sciences*, edited by Daniel Lerner and Harold D. Lasswell, Stanford University Press, Stanford, Calif., 1951, pp. 44–69.

minute operations. Rather than rushing to and fro seeking desperately to come up with a solution to a threatened strike or a ticklish grievance, he will be able to focus on the sources of these problems.

Perhaps we have come the full circle in the field of personnel relations. Some decades ago the easy assumption was made that the firm could maximize output by giving intelligent consideration only to the vital engineering considerations: layout, division and allocation of work, methods, scheduling, etc. Then a whole school of opponents developed with the motto, "People are not machines." They contended that factors like personal motivation, leadership, morale, and identification were much more important in contributing to high worker efficiency than the specifics of the engineering. The conflict of engineering versus human relations has raged ever since.

Yet the conclusions of this study indicate that the technology of the plant—the way jobs are distributed and flow into one another and the nature of the division of labor—molds the types of work groups that evolve within the plant. We have known with some assurance for more than twenty years, since the Western Electric studies, that the work group shapes the beliefs and behavior of its employee membership. Now it would appear that the technological structure of the organization, in turn, exerts a major influence on the source of motivation and morale, the work group. This is the reason for the statement that the field of personnel relations has come the full circle to the point where engineering considerations are once again crucial.

In brief, then, this study examines certain enduring extremes in plant-level industrial relations. There is special concentration on groups that were classified as "poor" in their behavior, for two reasons. Most importantly, this method seemed the strategic thing to do; the sore spots in an organization are more readily apparent, and where problems are sharply accented they are easier to study than the average or modal situation. Secondly, although in the collective bargaining area, conflict has always been a sufficiently attractive phenomenon to encourage research, in the broader field of personnel administration most studies have stressed "good supervision," "sound-management policies," "teamwork," and "organizational stability." We chose to give more attention to the tension areas.

Summary

We would expect the complex and dynamic character of the industrial plant to provide many sources of worker dissatisfaction. But, whereas the preponderance of research in the field of industrial relations has stressed the relevance of adequate methods of leadership, skillful tactics, and astute administrative procedures, we have observed that the *organization of work* contributes significantly to the behavior of work groups. The analysis of work group records furnished us by union and management officials indicates that we can predict which groups will challenge the actions of both management and the union and which will tend to accept their conditions of work and remuneration. The *methods* utilized by the group in making these challenges are also determinable. Insofar as we can show that certain behavior patterns are associated with identifiable work group types, our theories of supervisory selection and training and of the introduction of technological change undergo substantial revision. In the other direction, we can begin to consider the implications for employee behavior of particular engineering decisions which determine work flow and job arrangements.

With few exceptions our emphasis will be on behavior, on what these groups of employees actually do in the plant. We are much less concerned with what they think they would like to do, ought to do, or might have done. In contrast to the more typical emphasis on attitudes in a large proportion of industrial relations studies, we are concerned with action that is observable. Not only does the social scientist find the evidence of actual behavior easier to evaluate, but the administrator knows it is more crucial to the situation. Rather than concentrating on who likes whom and what and how much they like other people and policies, this study is concerned with what employees do about their relative likes and dislikes.

This then is a study of human relations in the industrial plant. Our conclusions, however, do not stress the accepted maxim that the best made plans of managers often go astray because of the human element. Quite the contrary: the human element, so-called, is a resultant of the technological decisions and, in part at least, predictable from them.

Management is often told that it must learn to work with "groups" since employees frequently do not respond as individuals. There is usually the tacit assumption that these groups are all alike. We are suggesting that the differences among work groups are more significant than their similarities. The differences include the methods these groups evolve to solve their day-to-day problems, their response to management and supervision, and the type of people they recognize as their leaders.

Based on our earlier studies of industrial organizations, the work group is the dynamic factor in shaping the critical pressures and decisions which determine the industrial relations climate of the plant. Our research seeks to explain this behavior and provide benchmarks for administrative action.

Plan of the Volume

The material that follows is based on field study data collected by the author during the period 1951–1955. The conclusions are derived from an examination of work records, interviews, and observations of 300 work groups in thirty plants in a variety of industries.[2]

The next chapter presents a number of cases to illustrate typical behavior patterns of the groups we observed. An analysis of the data appeared to disclose four rather distinctive patterns of work group behavior. These are illustrated and compared. It should be noted that these patterns are empirically derived "ideal types"; although certain clusters of variables reappear with high frequency, no single work group in the study necessarily exhibits all the characteristics of any one type.

The next and perhaps more important step is to answer the question, "Why do these differences exist and persist?" This problem is discussed in Chapter 3, which seeks to explain why these distinctions in group reactions to management and the union are maintained.

Chapter 4 is concerned with events within the plant that stimulate or set off aggressive behavior on the part of work groups, and with the possibilities for change in the basic patterns that have been identified.

The administrative implications for line managers, personnel executives, and union officials are explored in Chapter 5. A number of cherished beliefs are brought into question. The next chapter, 7, is devoted to the implications of this kind of work group data for the theories of the behavioral scientist dealing with groups in industry. The last chapter seeks to summarize the total study.

[2] A more complete description of the research method is contained in the Appendix.

chapter 2

Case descriptions of the four work group types

In this chapter we want the reader to sample the variety of work groups described to us by management and the union. (We had requested examples of groups that had been consistent in their behavior over relatively long periods of time, even through changes in supervision as well as management policies. The cases included should give some of the flavor of their actions in the plant. Also, the reader may be able to detect certain similarities, both in the type of behavior demonstrated and the technological characteristics of the groups involved.)

It will be observed that most of the qualities of the work groups described relate to their participation in the grievance process, as very broadly defined. That is, our observers in the plants, when referring to "hot spots" or "cooperative groups," placed most of their emphasis on the level of acceptance of and cooperation with management decisions, or, contrariwise, on the frequency and nature of the challenge issued by the group to management.

Usually we think of the degree of acceptance or rejection of management decisions as being primarily a function of union actions and supervisory effectiveness. However, in describing the plant, participants on both sides stressed the role of the work group itself and its propensity to accept or protest—the initiation of action upward.

In reality, this presentation is just the other side of the coin we usually examine when we are concerned about the degree of employee satisfaction and factors relating to it. In the day-to-day world of affairs, administrators are forced to concentrate on problem centers which demand their attention and absorb their energies. Thus, without saying that the absence of expressed discontent indicates high employee satisfaction, we believe that it is sometimes appropriate to direct research by the priority system used by the administrator. (At a later point we shall consider the relationship between observed expressions of employee dissatisfaction and what is typically referred to as "morale.")

As the data was accumulated and reviewed it appeared that what was being described to us was not one but a variety of work groups. These groups differed from one another very substantially, particularly in the way they dealt with any problems they faced. For the sake of convenience we have attached names to the four types most clearly distinguishable: the *Apathetic*, the *Erratic*, the *Strategic*, and the *Conservative*. It will be well to remember that the name is only a convenience, a shorthand method of referring to a set of distinguishing characteristics. The author believes that the connotation of each of these words is appropriate for the behavior demonstrated by the group in question; the reader, of course, is free to reject this appellation.

In the sections to follow, we shall attempt to describe the four basic work group types which became differentiated as our study progressed. We shall give examples that will highlight the essential qualities of the groups included under each of the general categories; and we shall attempt to provide some basis for assessing their common characteristics.

Type 1: The Apathetic Groups

By almost any measure these departments were the least likely to develop grievances or engage in concerted action as a means of pressuring management or the union. Although incidents did occur on occasion, compared with other groups these workers were disinclined to challenge decisions or attempt to gain something "extra" for themselves. Surprisingly, however, these departments were not ranked highest by management for their consistent productivity and "cooperativeness." Apparently the Apathetics were not trouble-free, but only superficially so. Put in another way, there was evidence of worker discontent, but often it was not focused in terms of specific demands or grievances.

These same groups were also less prone to engage in union politics and to participate in the internal life of their unions. Within these departments petty jealousies and interpersonal problems were somewhat more common than in the other groups. Although management and union representatives could identify certain influential members of the group, real leadership seemed to be dispersed among a relatively large number of individuals. Group cohesion, as such, did not seem to be a primary characteristic of these Apathetic groups.

Here are some examples:

The Hammershop. This department consisted of about fifty men and has not changed much in size during the last 30 years.

The work of the hammershop has few equals in terms of skill required and attendant dangers. The machines which the employees operate, the drop hammers, are tremendous brutes, representing tons of steel and high pressure. Whereas the village smith needed only his own skill and his fabled muscles to shape the metals he worked with, the hammershop crew must depend on the agility and strength of each member, all of whom do different jobs.

On the basis of the teamwork required to do the job and, moreover, in order to earn a satisfactory bonus, we expected the men to comprise a tightly knit group, but an examination of the department revealed quite the opposite. The men were divided within the crew unit itself and among crews. They had deep-seated dissatisfactions over their wages and working conditions. Over the years their relative earnings position in the plant had suffered significantly.

The union was discouraged with the department's failure to support its demands by specific action. It decried the department's lack of "self-control," for the men frequently finished jobs, having rates about which they had complained, in a relatively short period of time. On the other hand, easy jobs might be delayed interminably by petty frictions. These discrepancies in performance hurt the group's bargaining power.

The men admitted that "Every so often, we threaten the union by saying that we're going to walk out—but they know it's just an idle threat. We never do." Time after time the comment was heard, "The reason why we never get anything is that the men don't stick together." Some group in the department was usually blamed: the young men, the highly skilled hammersmiths, a crew which was unwilling to take responsibility, or perhaps the crew presumed to be the company's favorite. Still other explanations were put in terms of the environment outside the department—"After all, the union doesn't care, so what good does it do?" or "You know there's no point in walking out unless you're sure other departments in the plant are going to walk out too, and you never can really be sure of that, can you?"

The men felt the company favors the crew with the most skilled hammersmith by giving him the best equipment and the choicest jobs. Almost in the next breath they admitted that the quality of the work on that particular crew was superior, and the company "needs to keep them happy in order to get the really difficult jobs done that the rest of us can't handle." So there is recognition of both skill and prestige differences among the crews, since not all hammersmiths are equally competent; and these differences arouse jealousies.

It does not come as a surprise that the men in the department had been relatively inactive in nearly all union activities. Both their stewards were from the lowest paying jobs in the department, and they served without enthusiasm, anxious to quit but unable to find men willing to replace them. Each year they were, in effect, reappointed because there was no opposition.

In any work group there are differences in interest and points of view among the younger and older workers and the relatively more skilled and the relatively less skilled. Here, however, the crew form of organization, with its sharp distinctions in both rank and earnings, accented these differences. The hammershop had demonstrated to itself as well as to the union and management, that it did not have the basic unity necessary to conduct the kind of collective bargaining that other departments in the same plant were conducting. That this was an important shortcoming was apparent to a number of men in the department, who referred to their many failures and their evident weakness. Lacking common interests and economic strength, the men grew more disillusioned with the union, which in turn grew more disillusioned with them.

A Shipping Department. Interviews in this department disclosed that there were not even any informal groupings among the workers. The employees were young, both in seniority and chronological age. Many saw themselves as temporary employees. Often they worked in crews on unloading and loading operations. There was no one who could be called an "informal leader." Few took the jobs seriously enough to be concerned with improving working conditions through group action. A good deal of horseplay was observed, and a major supervisory problem is one of discipline. Most of the men did not know the name of their union representative.

This pattern repeated itself in the other shipping departments for which we had data. A wide variety of jobs and ratings are characteristic of these departments. Occasionally an outburst would take place, but it was short-lived. Many times the transfer of one or two employees or their leaving the department cleared up the trouble. Yet in these same departments management was disappointed over productivity, much as the union was disappointed over worker apathy.

Metal Disking. One characteristic operation in automobile body plants is metal disking. This is one of the early smoothing operations on the welded body which serves to begin the preparation for painting. The men handle heavy power tools, and the great quantity of metal dust and shavings produced requires that masks be worn at all times. They work in two parallel lines between which the auto bodies move on a conveyor on an assembly line basis. The operation is carried on in a shedlike enclosure, apart from the other body shop employees.

The work is considered dangerous as well as very unpleasant. When possible, men avoided assignments into the department. With the great amount of noise, the generally poor working conditions, and the relatively low rates paid (in terms of other jobs), we might have expected signs of aggressive behavior. Just the reverse was the case; work group disturbances were almost non-existent.

Punch Press Departments. The relatively low level of skill employed, the absence of any leeway in standards (few jobs are easier to time study), and the aura of fear surrounding the job (fear of catching hands or fingers in the presses) places serious limitations on the ability of a punch press department to exercise any real influence. The employees see their jobs as being unpopular in the plant community. As a result, we found only a few punch press departments that were problem centers, except in terms of productivity. Most of them were passive, or if disturbed, were so only for short periods.

Another job that fits this same general description, except that it lacks the danger factor is *drill press* work. Drill press groups are even more passive, however, in most of the cases we observed.

SUMMARY: THE APATHETIC GROUPS

These groups are not likely to challenge management or union decisions. While we shall want to explore more systematically at a later point the possible explanations of this pattern of in-plant behavior, certain common characteristics of the groups we have described are readily apparent. A number of the jobs included are relatively low skilled and low paid, particularly in terms of the general wage pattern of the plants in which they are located. The groups that do not fit this description are primarily performing operations that involve a degree of interworker cooperation. These include crew operations, such as the hammershop, where each member of the crew performs a different operation having a separate job classification. Press shop, electric furnace, enameling, and utility line crews fit this description as well—namely, having an interdependence of different jobs, infrequent grievance activity, and only sporadic union participation.

We use the term "crew" to refer to a group of employees dependent on one another to accomplish a common work task. The crew differs from the assembly operation, the other type of interdependent work situation to which we shall refer, in that the members all interact with one another in the work process. The assembly line, on the other hand, involves a chain of interaction: *A* with *B*, *B* with *A* and *C*, *C* with *B* and *D*, etc., as its flow of work. We found *long* assembly lines, typical in many industries, also behaving like Apathetic groups. These lines tie together large numbers of workers in a progressive flow-of-work.

Although no typical cases have been cited, it should also be mentioned that work departments where each employee performs a different function, utilizing distinctive equipment—a "mixed department" in our terminology—appear to fit into the general category of Apathetic groups. These departments do not utilize a significant number of multiples of any given machine or skill. Such a department, for example, would include machining, assembling, and testing operations. (These are frequently examples of work organization on an integrated or product basis as contrasted to a functional organization, e.g., all punch press operations in one location.) In such groups common grievances are relatively infrequent, as are other types of group action. While there is a "social group" and there may be a "work team," there is unlikely to be any concerted action by the members. Certainly a few areas of common concern remain; supervision is one. But overall, the number of common denominators is limited and, therefore, so is the incentive for group action. One infrequently finds such areas being trouble spots or centers for antiunion or antimanagement behavior.

The behavior characteristics of the Apathetic group are:

1. Relatively few grievances or use of pressure tactics.
2. Lack of clearly identified or accepted leadership.
3. Internal disunity and frictions.
4. Evidence of suppressed discontent.

Type II: The Erratic Groups

The most distinctive characteristic of some work groups was their tendency toward "erratic" behavior. By this statement is meant that there seems to be no relation between the seriousness of their grievances (from the point of view of the employees themselves) and the intensity of their protests. Issues that both management and union observers consider minor, that is, problems which probably could be settled to the group's satisfaction by a brief discussion, might erupt without warning into a major conflagration—a mass demonstration of some kind, such as a wildcat strike. At the same time, deep-seated grievances may exist within these groups over long periods with no apparent reaction in terms of group behavior. Union leaders have suffered consistently because of this type of "split personality." Petty grievances often become nearly insoluble problems because of rash strikes and demonstrations. Many important cases languish in the grievance procedure because there is no support from the rank and file for their officers' efforts to convince management that "the men really feel this is very important to them."

In many ways such behavior is analogous to that described by the psychologists as being characteristic of frustration in the individual. The groups may be exhibiting a type of "fixation." The kinds of activities they indulge in are not contrived to solve their problems. Emotional reaction to some deep frustration has blinded them to their failure to adjust their reactions to circumstances. As a result they have stubbornly behaved in ways best designed to *defeat* their own objectives. Such irrational approach contrasts sharply with the keen tactical sense of the strategic groups discussed next.[1]

This explosiveness is matched by a management evaluation that places such groups at the top of the plant "very dangerous" list. In fact, a great deal of the time and energy of both management and union officials that is devoted to the grievance procedure is concentrated on these tension areas. Even so, the managers and union leaders often admitted frankly that they were at a loss to understand what was "really going on" in such departments. "You just don't know what to expect," was a typical descriptive assessment.

There was some scattered evidence that these kinds of groups are

[1] Cf. Norman Maier's discussion of frustration-instigated behavior as it applies to human relations in industry, in *Psychology in Industry*, Houghton Mifflin, Boston, 1946, pp. 67–79.

subject to rather sudden "conversions"—a department that had been a source of endless grief to all concerned became, literally overnight, one of the showplaces of the plant, where unanimity and harmony prevailed, and then perhaps at some later time, reverted back to its earlier condition.

In some instances, due, perhaps, to their ready inflammability, these groups occupied positions of leadership in the union during the early organizational phase, when emphasis was on the ability to rally immediate, aggressive support for the union leadership. In later years, when more mature skills of bargaining and strategic patience were prerequisites, top union positions were filled by representatives of other departments.

Internally these groups followed highly autocratic leadership that would "keep them in line," either in support of management objectives or in direct defiance of the rules. Unlike some of the more complex groups we shall deal with, the leadership in these departments was usually clear-cut and centralized—the same "strong" individual often served as the internal social leader and the external representative to union and to management. Some typical cases follow.

The Tub Polishers. This was a relatively large department in a company manufacturing heavy household appliances. A major metal component of one of the appliances, prior to a change in manufacturing processes, required vigorous hand polishing with simple tools. In a sense, this job was a type of assembly operation in which each man had almost identical tasks. The tubs moved along a line of men, through various stages of polishing (with appropriate differences in the tooling) from rough to final finishing. Each man performed a task, similar but not identical to his neighbor's. Primarily, the job tapped physical strength, although judgment was required in the finishing stages.

The hundred men in this department were considered the source of countless problems by the management. One problem led to another and not even a semipermanent solution seemed to be forthcoming. For example, the employees requested a change to a department-wide incentive plan. When this program was installed, replacing the individual piecework system that had been in effect, a sitdown strike followed. The management then broke the department down into smaller groups for the purpose of still another type bonus plan.

The internal organization of the department seemed primitive in comparison with other departments in the plant. When some difficulty arose the men insisted on crowding en masse into the superintendent's office. Under these circumstances, discussion of the problem at hand was impossible; everyone talked and shouted at once.

Frequent work stoppages occurred as long as the department was in existence. Often the reason for the stoppage was unknown. The men worked hard and grieved hard. Management referred to them as being "rough and tough." In many ways the department responded like a gang or even mob to work problems that developed, and its members seemed to savor work interruption with the accompanying trouble for its own sake. Observers deduced no specific sources of long-run discontent. They only saw day-to-day frictions of the most volatile kind.

Wet Sanders. A similar kind of occupational group, this one in the automobile industry, is the wet sanding group. These men, usually about a dozen per shift, work in the body shops that fabricate the non-mechanical shell of the car. At one stage—after welding, solder filling, disking (already described), and metal finishing—the so-called "body-in-white" is literally attacked by a small group of men wielding special abrasive papers that require large quantities of water to work effectively. Several such sanding groups are stationed on the line to finish every body, prior to the painting operations. The job is physically tedious, much like tub polishing, but does not require the same lifting operations. It is unpleasant as well, due to the necessity of working in water and with abrasive materials. Skill-wise, this job is relatively low on the automobile plant's occupational ladder.

The wet sand groups in many such plants were a source of continuous trouble, often resulting in work stoppages over a trivial matter. At times, they struck, not over a current issue, but for fear they would not get what they deserved in the future. The management considered this a concentration spot for trouble makers. In some plants the wet sanders had a high concentration of grievances, in others they ranked below average, but the inconsistency of their behavior was universally characteristic—slight difficulties causing explosions.

Strippers. The major job duty of these men is to strip off the selvage left on carton forms by the presses that die cut the forms from cardboard sheets. The surplus material is stripped from the piles of embossed cardboard sheets by a small crew of four to six men who work with the press crew. Again, this is a physically taxing job; the labor is primarily hand labor, and the tools are very simple ones.

Interestingly, the informal leader of the department is usually found within this group, although the men who operate the presses which emboss the cardboard are substantially more skilled than the strippers, with greater seniority, pay, and prestige.

There is high turnover in the department, which is considered one of the plant hot spots. As one company official put it, "If there is any place that you will get opposition to a company program, even a charity campaign, it is right here among the strippers." A grievance in another department will often induce the strippers to walk off the job, although the sudden decision to demonstrate can often be as quickly quelled by adept management action. The department manager was convinced, "Whenever we get rid of one radical in this department, we always get another."

Even though membership in these crews changes over time, the men as a group are highly unified in their struggle for certain benefits. (It is interesting to note that the press crew, which works with the strippers, exhibits the behavior of an Apathetic group; here the jobs are highly differentiated.)

Now shifting the scene to a completely different industry (copper refining) we have some evidence that in a technologically similar operation, stripping thin sheets of purified metal from forms, the crews involved exhibited almost identical behavior. They were highly volatile and vigorous in demanding a range of generous benefits to themselves. Ready to fight "at the drop of a hat," these homogeneous crews had the reputation for unbridled bellicosity which won them a loose incentive plan providing very high pay and the right to leave their jobs much earlier than their fellow workers.

Plating. This is almost a borderline operation between the Apathetic and Erratic types, as we have described them. In several plants the men who loaded and unloaded the racks that go through the electrochemical tanks were almost nonentities, completely apathetic in their behavior. The job was unpopular, having almost no skill associated with it; in addition, there was the unpleasantness of working near the fumes and drippings of caustic liquids. On occasion, the plating crews were trouble spots, particularly where the operation was a bottleneck in terms of maintaining plant operations. Many of the problems were petty gripes and interpersonal frictions, particularly between inspection and the rest of the plating crew. Also, technical difficulties which caused excessive work spoilage further shortened tempers and placed pressure on the situation. Productivity difficulties were a function of both unsolved technical problems and human relations.

In one of the plating departments an almost unbelievable transformation took place. A new steward was elected, who, upon taking office, assumed the responsibility of "keeping the workers in line." Since this bloodless revolution there have been no more complaints or production difficulties emanating from the department.

In another plating group, which continuously caused difficulties in the same plant, there were sudden spurts of cooperativeness that sometimes resulted in a temporary doubling of production. For example, on the basis of a wager with one of the management staff, the group evolved a nearly perfect pattern of production that succeeded in overcoming many of the inherent technical problems in the process. The men made countless adjustments, uncalled for by their job descriptions, that succeeded in making the process function as no engineer had been able to do.

It should be pointed out that these plating groups did not, from the point of view of management at least, engage in extended concerted activities. They grumbled and fought, but they did not permit many formal grievances, nor was it conceivable that they would engage in prolonged slowdowns or walkouts. However, their grievances were very time-consuming for both management and the union.

Other Erratics. A number of other groups exhibited behavior similar to that described above, and had similar technical characteristics. Many small assembly lines, where some skill and training were required behaved erratically. For example, packaging lines, particularly where these operations were more desirable jobs than the immediately preceding processing operations, were high grievance, "inflammable" areas. Many of these short assembly lines (typically, with five to twelve employees) functioned much like crews; the operators worked closely together and interacted with the entire group, not just with those stationed immediately next to them, as was true of the longer assembly lines.

Also, what might be referred to as "blind" interrelated work areas seemed tension-ridden. These were operations on which one group of operators were required to coordinate their activities with another group, with whom they could not communicate directly. One example is from a food processing plant. Material flowed between two stations located on separate floors, and because the process was not completely automatized, the receiving group had a number of adjustments to make if the incoming products came "too fast" or "too slow." Similarly, in an electric appliance plant, the metal cover was processed by one unit located a floor above those who were working on the internal mechanism. At the point at which the cover was dropped by a conveyor onto the semi-completed machine, perfect coordination was required. Models differed in their cover requirements and the operation of the assembly line required that the right cover come down the chute at just the right moment. However, as in the case of the two food processing stations, neither group could see the other; communications were entirely by mechanical means.

In each case supervisors correlated internal, intergroup disturbances with more traditional grievances. That is, when for one reason or another the two "halves" of the process were irritated with one another because of technical difficulties of coordination, it could be expected that within a short period of time one or both groups would press grievances against management, although the subjects of the complaints might have nothing to do with the internal bickerings.

As one member of the management described the timing:

> Every so often, the men upstairs loading the cover conveyor get smart and load a whole lot of them on, filling it up, and then complain that the men downstairs aren't taking them off fast enough. The next thing we know the men on the machine line are speeding up and using up covers at such a fast rate that they begin yelling about the cover men falling behind and not sending down an adequate supply. When this happens, we also begin getting complaints about working conditions, job standards and all the rest.

SUMMARY: THE ERRATIC GROUPS

These were primarily jobs in which everyone has an identical, or nearly identical task. Most significantly, in this category there was a high preponderance of groups in which workers are required to interact with one another by the work process. These crews and assembly lines, however, differed from those we often found exhibiting behavior that would cause them to be included in our Apathetic classification. Rather, these were homogeneous crews and short assembly lines in which job descriptions and rates matched nearly perfectly. Many of the jobs involved operations which are primarily worker controlled as distinct from machine controlled.

The behavior characteristics of the Erratic groups are:

1. Easily inflamed.
2. Poorly controlled pressure tactics, behavior inconsistent.
3. Quick conversions to good relationships with management.
4. Often highly centralized leadership.
5. Active in organizational phase of union.

Type III: The Strategic Groups

In many plants, one or two groups seemed to be at the very center of most of the really important grievances, important in the sense of involving major economic considerations. Often these groups were also a part of the core of the union "regulars," who kept close track of how well their specific economic interests were being advanced by the officers. Time after time, they succeeded in electing one of their number to top union office, even when they only comprised a small fraction of the membership. These were not the departments characterized by sudden flashes of activity. Rather, they seemed to be shrewdly calculating pressure groups which never tired of objecting to unfavorable management decisions, seeking loopholes in existing policies and contract clauses that would redound to their benefit, and comparing their benefits with those of other departments in the plant. They demanded constant attention for their problems and had the ability to reinforce their demands by group action.

Unlike the Erratic work groups, however, the amount and kind of pressure the Strategic groups exert are carefully measured, both against the objectives they seek and the immediate strategy of the total situation. Thus, only if surprise is chosen from the many weapons in their arsenal, is management shocked at a sudden display of aggression. Much like a thespian, they can "turn it on" or "turn it off" (where "it" refers to concerted activities such as slowdowns) as the occasion demands. To that degree, their behavior is predictable, and this consistency is seen as a virtue, both by management and the union. In fact, these work areas ranked substantially above the Apathetic and Erractic groups in general plant performance and cooperation.

We have selected the term *strategic* for these groups, to emphasize their ability to adapt their pressure tactics to the situation and to engage in sustained and carefully thought out wars of attrition with both management and the union. The appellation does not refer to the location of the group in the plant or in the production flow. It is a behavioral description to which we have reference here, and not an attribute.

The departments so classified seemed highly cohesive. The leadership consisted of a small core of highly active and influential group members, each of whom specialized in such functions as dealing with management, dealing with the union, maintaining internal unity, or taking the lead in voicing dissatisfaction.

The Polishers. Metal polishers have the reputation of being an elite group throughout the Detroit metalworking and automobile industry. The work is highly paid and considered relatively skilled, although it bears little resemblance to the traditional crafts in which apprenticeships are served. The jobs are performed by individual workmen using stationary or portable polishing wheels. Work standards, whether applied to incentive payment systems or measured daywork, are considered very loose. A typical reason given by management informants is that the final finishing operation on metals requires a critical judgment factor that cannot be time-studied precisely. Only experience and the operators immediate knowledge can determine in the final analysis how many passes are required or how long the metal must remain in contact with the polishing apparatus. Managers reported that in Detroit, an unaffiliated polishers' union was active in the early 1930's, years before any significant number of other production workers in automobile plants were organized.

Even where technological improvements have reduced the required skill, groups of polishers tend to maintain themselves as a skilled craft. Serious negotiation problems are posed by their demands for pay differentials greater than those granted to similar semiskilled occupational groups. Even when these demands are not granted, their equivalent may be incorporated in more lenient work standards that result in increased earnings or reduced effort.

In one large automobile plant with a reputation for vigorous management action, the polishers were the core of the original organizational efforts. While they comprised only about 5 per cent of the total production force, they have elected local union presidents and consistently have elected one of the more active shop committeemen. This group, numbering about 300 employees, has been the center of resistance to new work standards whenever new automobile models are introduced. The standards disputes drag on interminably, primarily through the ability of the group to "hold the line" on resisting changes. While the management is very proud of its firm policy on all concerted slowdowns or stoppages, the polishers have been able to hold their production to one-half of management established work standards for several months before settling on a new, mutually acceptable rate of output. The same drawnout procedure, which, in the words of one superintendent, ". . . saves them a couple months of effort every year," is repeated annually.

Perhaps one wildcat walkout in this plant is an interesting testimonial to the kind of forces involved. Several informal leaders started a walkout over the issue of inoperative ventilating fans. The fans had been shut down for routine cleaning purposes, although the department was kept operating due to the heavy pressure of back orders. The superintendent, detecting the incipient stoppage, immediately ordered the fans to be turned back on and the cleaning operation postponed. However, the walkout continued when the informal leaders announced that management had attempted to keep a committeeman from coming into the department. A picket line established outside the gate kept a large percentage of the next shift from reporting to work as well. By the end of that next day, however, the top union leadership had succeeded in getting the men back to work.

In recent years, two out of six major wildcat strikes in the company started in this department.

The company described the current formal leader of the department, the elected committeeman, as a conservative, restrained official, a tough but reasonable person. Management estimates that about 1 per cent of the department is actually active in the department's informal leadership. (We have observed in other studies that, for the union as a whole, not more than 1 per cent is usually active in pressing grievances and participating in the collective bargaining process.) The group is thought to be "highly legalistic" and "very picky about every little question."

Significantly, one autoworker union official noted that at another plant the polishers are losing strength as changes in the operation cause them to be scattered, rather than concentrated in a single location, although they now hold the local presidency.

Grievances from the buffing group (a somewhat similar, but less skilled occupation than polishing), are "taken with a grain of salt" by management, and they do not compare in number and severity to those of the polishers.

The Engine Block Chippers. Both the job and job behavior of this group were very similar to those of the skilled metal finishers. The chippers worked on engine blocks in a large foundry, using a wide variety of small hand tools to remove molding imperfections from the blocks. While this foundry of 1,000 men employed mass production methods, each block was slightly different, from the point of view of the chipping.

Although there were only thirteen men classified in the job, they dominated the plant in every way. They were a continual source of grievances, although they had gradually worked their earnings up to the highest level in the plant. Their job was individual and had important judgment features. No time-study man could contradict the worker who said he had to use three or four extra tools and motions to get in and through some of the core holes and inside the block. Their production standards were the most liberal in the plant. This situation was reflected in their ability to start a half hour later than other workers, finish a half hour earlier, and still earn over $30 per day. From management's point of view they had the union "wrapped up" as well and few dared refuse their never-ending stream of demands. Although from all outward signs their concerted activities had been enormously successful, they never tired of new demands. Further, they periodically shut down the plant by well timed strikes, when their demands were not met.

It is interesting to note that the men worked in the same room on individual operations, that is, without worker interdependence, in an essentially crew-based technology (a foundry).

The Wire Drawers. A relatively common occupational group in many plants associated with the steel industry are the wire drawers. These men, singly or in pairs, operate one or a number of semi-automatic machines that reduce the size of metal wire by pulling it through a series of dies. The operators' major responsibilities are starting up the machine (a threading process), removing finished rolls, and maintaining the process by catching breakdowns or potential breakdowns.

In several of the mills studied these were, by any measure, the most active departments in the grievance process. The men were always conscious of company discrimination; their perpetual complaint, "We're not getting our share." Management felt that the men had "too much time to think," and that they used this machine time (when no substantial amount of operator attention was required) to muse obsessively about working conditions. Because their job status was only medium high, and their job classification relatively low for steel operations, they were often unsuccessful in their demands. However, in terms of number of grievances, they were unsurpassed by the more highly skilled steelmakers in the plant.

A good example of wire drawer independence and self-confidence was provided by a recent case reported by a union international representative. The plant in question employed about fifty men classified as wire drawers. Incentive earnings were very generous, as the men themselves recognized, and their jobs were the envy of the remainder of the production force in the plant. Recently the company had obtained a much sought-after customer's order that required seven-day operations. The contract permitted management-initiated changes in schedules and shifts; but the wire drawers, against the advice of their union, resisted Saturday and Sunday work that would not be paid for at premium rates. Considering the existing high earnings level of the group and their union agreement which made no provision for these premium rates, neither local officials nor fellow workers were sympathetic with the extended slowdown started by the wire drawers.

For two months the men sacrificed all incentive earnings. Their continued resistance threatened the loss of the new contract and the additional jobs it would provide. Their strength and confidence made union support largely unnecessary, if not superfluous.

Truckers. In many industrial plants, the in-plant truckers form one of the more important occupational groups. These men operate small lift and tow trucks. In the automobile industry, large trailers are often utilized to haul bodies to the motor and chassis line (between plants). The critical importance of the work they do is unquestioned; in most instances regular delivery of raw materials and the hauling away of the semifinished product from each processing station are indispensable to continuous operations. They also move goods into and out of warehouse storage. The job descriptions are almost identical for most truckers. Their unique mobility for the industrial plant, and the manifest skills and stamina involved in their work develop a real *esprit de corps* in the group.

However, their status in the plant is not unchallenged. Management as well as fellow workers sometimes have the impression that "anyone can drive one of those trucks with a few hours' practice." Work standards are also ambiguous. Not only are many operations unsupervised because of the far-flung operations involved, but slight variations in the ordering of the flow can cause major differences in the time requirements on such jobs as stacking and unstacking. These ambiguities provide a fruitful field for concerted effort on the part of the group to improve job conditions, wage rates, and relative benefits.

In nearly every plant we found truckers highly active in asserting their rights and in seeking new rights. They are a power in the union and in the plant. Management rarely complained of their output, however, only about their bellicosity.

Grinders. There are a number of production machines designed to surface metal parts by a grinding process. The jobs involved vary in skill, depending on the exact type of machine utilized and on whether or not the operator is required to set up the machine or merely to operate the equipment (insert stock, observe it during processing, and remove the finished pieces). Nearly always, the work is more skilled than operating simple power machines, such as drill and punch presses, and less skilled, for example, than certain lathe and screw machine work. Most grinder work is characterized by some element of judgment, although tolerances are usually closely controlled. After the machine is set up and running, the operator, who works as an individual, usually has some free time to engage in conversation with fellow workers.

In every plant observed, with one exception, a concentration of grinder machine operators was regarded as a high grievance activity area, both in production departments and toolrooms (where the men regrind production tools to maintain their cutting efficiency). Grinders[2] were consistent and often successful candidates for top union positions, although they usually comprised only a small percentage of the total membership. They rarely engaged in actual work stoppages; rather, they concentrated on well-thought out (although not necessarily justifiable) grievances that challenged management standards and authority. Often the grievance period extended over a period of years—they never gave up on an important case. When a case was lost, it would reappear in another grievance in slightly altered form.

Leadership was often diffuse. Management recognized that the men who were the spokesmen (and most outspoken) were not necessarily the real social leaders who organized the internal solidarity and helped frame the goals of the group. Our studies of the internal life of one such grinder group confirmed this observation; the group was led by a leadership clique that included an external contact man, an agitator and a social leader.[3]

Hand Screw Machine Operators. In one plant there was a large concentration of hand screw machines that were, in fact, the major production machine, aside from the substantially lesser skilled punch presses, drill presses, and milling machines. Men on these latter machines had no illusion (or delusion) about the skill required to operate their equipment or the appropriateness of their classification. However, the hand screw operators consistently felt "underevaluated." Management, they believed, had no conception of the skills required in their type of work. Although their jobs required no interworker

[2] It is interesting to note that tool sharpeners and tool grinders are one of the lowest skilled occupational groups in the high skill toolrooms.

[3] Leonard Sayles, "A Case Study of Union Participation and Technological Change," *Human Organization*, XI, 1952, pp. 5–15.

cooperation, their grievance activities did require group action. On almost every conceivable subject they registered grievances and initiated walkouts, with the greatest concentration in the wage differential area.

On the other hand, in plants where there were grinders, in substantial numbers, and where a limited number of hand screw machines were considered "high skill" machines, management did not experience this steady run of grievances. In such plants the hand screw machine operators were near the top of the prestige ladder, not in the middle as they were when they demonstrated the behavior characteristics of strategic groups.

Welders. Here is an occupational group that in most plants is synonymous with a high level of self-interest activity. In plant after plant the same story was repeated: the welders were a group that never tired of efforts to improve their own position, of seeking the slightest flaws in management behavior, and of making themselves the center for grievance activity.

Welding work varies in skill; in general, the type to which we have reference is the non-automatic variety that requires judgment and some learning period. Nearly all the work is done on an individual operator basis. Observers often conflict in their assessment of the real skill required of the welder and this ambiguity is one of the telltale characteristics of these highly active groups. They lack the assurance of the real crafts. In many plants, supervisors liked to brag they could train an average welder within a few weeks or months. The welders were usually identified as a "devil-may-care" group, highly cohesive and willing to go to great lengths to obtain that to which they think they are entitled, or would like to become entitled.

We found here, as in the other Strategic groups, an important judgment factor in the job. Both welders and their supervisors agreed that the welder himself controls much of the time spent on each job. If management sets a "tight" standard, the welder can "turn up the torch." However, if management does request this degree of heat intensity, thus shortening the time required for a given job, the welder can "prove" that it only damages the work. Apparently, good welders can set their own pace, and time studies have little impact upon them.

To really appreciate the position of the welders in some plants which they dominate, we have transcribed some interviews in a manufacturing plant of about 1,500 employees, which, at the time of the study, employed approximately 150 welders. These are some of the things the welders told us:

WELDER A: We would never permit any of our jobs to be restudied. We wouldn't take none of that bull from the time-study department. They pull that stuff with some of the groups, but they never pull it off with the welders. We would walk out on them.

WELDER B: You bet the welders built up the union. If the others want to take that sort of thing (from management) it's up to them. One thing is clear and that is the welders can get things done. For example, when other workers get base rate on a job, we get average hourly earnings. The company knows we can tie up the whole plant in a day or two and they better not play around with us.

WELDER C: We've stuck together as a group whenever we wanted anything and we've fought for it. A number of times on walkouts and sit-downs we've left the rest of the plant at work. Why are we so united? Maybe it's because whatever sort of work we're doing, if it's welding, it's almost identical, while men on most machines differ by a little bit. We always have every job down pat and know just what we can do on it. We learned when we were on individual piece rates; every man makes sure he knows what he is earning, how fast he should do the job, etc. With the other groups, it's different; most of them leave it up to the gang leader.

WELDER D: We're almost a union by ourselves. If anything goes wrong, we tell the company if they don't come down and settle this by such and such a time, we're not going to do any more of this work. The other groups just aren't as united.

Other men in the plant shared the same conclusions concerning the strength and self-confidence of the welders, although there was often a note of sarcasm in their comments:

Of course, if you talk to them, they'll tell you they're the whole plant. Maybe they are, because unless you're a welder, you're crazy to go above forty per cent of base on your incentive.

The welders are always patting each other on the back. They get around a lot, kid each other, and have a lot of spirit. Other fellows, like machine operators, stick to their own jobs and keep by themselves most of the time, and many of the men are thrown around so much they don't know where they're going to work next—but the welders—they're always right in there.

The self-assurance and bravado of the welders cannot be overstressed. These feelings help assure them *they possess* the needed strength to achieve their objectives. The benefits they win, in turn, reflect their cohesiveness.

Pressers. In the men's and women's clothing industry, the pressers have a job which most closely resembles the typical "hard goods" machine operator's job. Pressing machines are placed closely together in rows and are operated by individual employees. Where the work is not mechanized, each presser wields the familiar iron, much like a metal finisher uses a sanding wheel.

In most companies, management has come to respect the solidarity and negotiating strength of the pressers. They are ever ready to initiate a grievance, and their internal strength usually assures them at least partial victory. In plant prestige and in earnings, they usually rank just below the cutters. However, the rare and sought-after skills of the cutters are of such undeniable importance, that they rarely have to struggle for their demands, as we shall see in the next section.

Others too have observed the grievance proneness of the pressers. Chandler's description is from her study of several plants manufacturing women's clothing:

> [In one of the factories] . . . the pressers were generally regarded as the strongest group of piece rate workers. . . . They were well known for their ability to stick together, and management claimed that the pressers had more slowdowns and more sitdowns than any other group. . . .[4]

> [In another case] While the activities of the workers in the other departments were largely confined to the covert level, the pressers' activities often erupted into full-scale conflict with management. The pressers were the leading worker group in the factory. It was they who first devised new modes of worker behavior . . . Almost all of the important grievance cases between union and management are in the pressing department.[5]

Almost without exception, the pressers have this kind of reputation throughout the clothing industry.

WITHIN THE AUTOMOBILE INDUSTRY

A group of occupations, or perhaps more realistically, job classifications, in the automobile industry do not fit perfectly into the Strategic framework. Such jobs as metal finisher, torch solderer, trimmer and cushion builder (actual terminology will vary among

[4] Margaret Chandler, *Labor-Management Relations in Illini City, Case Study 3: Garment Manufacture*, University of Illinois, Institute of Labor and Industrial Relations, Champaign, Ill., 1953, p. 483.

[5] *Ibid.*, pp. 474–475.

the several major manufacturers) appear *to fit between* our Strategic groups and our Erratic groups. All of these jobs are found in the body shops, not in motor assembly plants. There are a number of operators concentrated in each of these classifications. In terms of the average skill in the industry, these are relatively skilled jobs, and in many instances management would have difficulty in placing untrained employees immediately on them.[6] Over the years, the jobs have gained an aura of skill, due to the efforts of the employees themselves to a substantial extent. For example, in trimming and cushion building, management has substituted easily operated staplers for the traditional tools of the upholsterer, tacks and hammers. Through their union, men in these classifications have resisted reduced rate classifications for such jobs, insisting that substantial skill differentials still separate them from the assembler, the largest and most inclusive job classification.

Unlike our other examples of Strategic groups, which are primarily individual jobs, these men work "on the line." With the exception of the cushion builders, they all work on the main assembly line on which the automobile body is constructed. The cushion builders work on a subassembly line which fabricates the automobile seat cushions.

The industrial relations record of these groups is literally filled to overflowing with wildcat strikes and slowdowns. Detroit newspapers, with unbelievable regularity, carry stories of how a dozen workmen in one of these departments succeeded in shutting down an entire plant employing 10,000 to 15,000 persons. Of course the very nature of the assembly operation makes it highly susceptible to these kinds of disturbances, in which a very small stoppage shuts down the entire process. A progressive assembly line depends on the continuous effort of every group, and with union discipline prohibiting the filling of strikers' jobs, even wildcat strikes not officially recognized by the union can be effective.

It is significant that the great majority of such stoppages seem to occur in just these particular work areas. To be sure, statistical confirmation is lacking. Neither management nor union publicizes or even reveals to the researcher the exact totals, because wildcat stoppages and slowdowns flaunt company and union discipline.[7]

However, data such as this is probably representative. In one

[6] However, these workers receive only five cents more per hour than the assemblers—the most numerous occupational group in the industry.

[7] Leonard R. Sayles, "Wildcat Strikes," *Harvard Business Review,* XXXII, 1954, pp. 48–50.

plant of a major producer, 40 out of 75 plant stoppages in the past several years have been directly attributable to the actions of the trimmers!

In terms of plant prestige and status, these groups are above the average of most Erratic groups observed. However, their activities seem much less restrained than those of the Strategic groups. In many ways, the pace of the industrial relations life of these automobile industry groups approximates their work pace. Modern technology and management have made the automobile assembly plant a highly dynamic processing unit. Continuous noise, the sparks and smoke of the welder and solderer, and the heat of hundreds of other small and large power tools forming the finished automobile provide the perfect picture of mass-production methods. The same pace is maintained in the grievance process: the time lag between these groups' consciousness of an inequity and their direct action against it is reduced to almost zero.

Metal Finishers. Closely related occupationally to the polishers described previously are the metal finishers. These men use a variety of hand tools (such as files) to improve the surface quality of machined, welded, and pressed sheet metal. They are considered slightly more skilled than the polishers and also slightly less troublesome. In fact, they are among the highest paid of the non-craft production groups in the Detroit automobile industry. Both on and off the assembly lines, metal finishing is considered one of the best production jobs. It is one of the few jobs on the production line which company spokesmen consider skilled. Even on motor-driven assembly lines, when dissatisfied, the group is able to execute the perfect slowdown, whereby each man slows down the same amount and all gradually move out of position.

At one large automobile plant the metal finishers consistently elect local presidents as well as shop chairmen. They feel that the quality of the finished product (the appearance of the car) is in large measure determined by their efforts. The group is considered very astute, and therefore top management feels that it takes an extremely competent supervisor to manage the department. In fact, metal finishers have a reputation for "finishing" foremen.

Trim Department. The most bellicose of these groups, however, are the trimmers. Most of their work consists in installing the "soft goods," such as wind hose, door pads, and headliners, inside the chassis. This work traditionally was done with the upholsterer's hammer and tacks. To be able to mouth a relatively large number of steel tacks and spit them singly onto the head of the magnetized hammer and then, almost in the same motion, drive them into some upholstering fabric was considered a highly skilled operation. The mark or symbol of their trade, still referred to in the shops, was this very "tack spitting." Today the stapler gun eliminates most of the skill involved but the trimmers are still conscious of their distinctiveness in working with cloth in an industry dominated by metal. One of the trim foremen observed:

> With steel, it either fits or it doesn't; but cloth is another matter. It takes a good man to know just how much it should stretch and how much it shouldn't, and to fit it into place with just the right amount of tension. There is no tool that can do that . . . only the experienced hand of a good trimmer. That's why you can never make an unskilled operation out of trimming.

Of course, this characteristic has complicated the setting of work standards and has made grievances a more attractive possibility. In a real sense the trimmers continue to think of themselves as upholsterers, and they share the pride of the furniture upholsterer, who is a self-assured craftsman.

Many higher company officials are pleased with the changes in the job, asserting that now the trimmers who walk out on illegal strikes can be replaced; they are no longer indispensable. However, the changes in the job, that is, the subdivision of the original operation into a larger number of simplified tasks and the development of the stapling method, have not changed in any basic fashion the behavior of the trimming group.

Most of these changes took place in the late forties, but the trimmers are as aggressive and feared as ever throughout the automobile industry. While management believes that the new method of trimming makes their work comparable to other work classified as assembling, the trimmers still receive a differential in pay over the assemblers. In addition, their high propensity to strike continues. The stage has been reached where responsible union officials were willing to admit that the trimmers carry their demands to excess. An autoworker international representative exclaimed with conviction:

> Many of them now don't do anything approximating a day's work. It is embarrassing for us sometimes to try to negotiate a new rate for them when they are only working half as hard as most of the men in the body shop. Some of them don't know what it is any more to put in a day's work.

In many ways the trim group represents the apocryphal powder keg. Management representatives frequently observe what they call "tail ending" in disputes. That is, a dispute in one section of the trim department will touch off a whole series of unrelated grievances. This upsetting rash of complaints may keep personnel and union relations people tied up for many weeks.

In part, this contagion in the dispute process may reflect the physical structuring of the work. Typically within the trim department, the work stations are crowded together, bringing men from the various trim groups into close physical proximity. An additional factor is the tendency for the assembly line to "snake" through the department in such a way that groups that would otherwise not be close together are working back to back. In some companies, at least, there is a direct relation between physical proximity and grievance contagion.

Two other characteristics of the department are of significance. Within the department a substantial number of tension incidents occur with some degree of regularity. One supervisor noted that a great number of fights take place among the men. Perhaps related to this, an examination of candidates for union office indicated an unusually large number of office seekers among the trimmers. Unlike the typical plant department, where one or perhaps two men oppose one another for the position of department steward, the trim department often produces five or six candidates. Also, trim groups, while they are highly active, do not seem to produce successful presidential candidates in the local. They elect fewer officers than their overall level of activity would lead one to expect.

It is significant that the trim group as a whole rarely is involved in a direct dispute with management or the union. It is the various smaller groups that comprise the trim department, each numbering typically from two to ten men doing a similar operation, who engage in grievance activity and slowdowns. Management claims that they cannot detect any mutual support for one another's grievances. The tail ending is not seen as mutual support but rather, as mutual inflammation—the sight of one group taking action fires others to do the same. The most serious conflicts occur where two important trim groups are working next to one another.

The data imply that the problems in the department are aggravated by the number of distinct centers of group formation. In other departments the impression was gained that the individual group reacts much like the total plant: a number of disputes are focused in a single major conflict that may result in a strike. However, the strike itself, once terminated, has served to "clear the air"; antagonisms have been expressed and the result is substantially better feelings than existed before the battle. Such a result cannot occur when the issues and disputes are fractionated as they are in the trim department. There each dispute serves only to arouse neighboring groups to the possibilities of concerted action.

Usually a dispute involving one group causes a shutdown of the department or plant with accompanying pay loss to all persons involved. As a result there might be an incentive on the part of those who did not initiate the strike to get something for themselves in the next walkout. This consideration suggests the possibility that a deposit system exists: for each block of lost time that is sustained when one group is engaged in a dispute, a credit is gained that may be expended at some future time to cause others to lose earnings.

To summarize, the trimmers resembled other Strategic group departments in their sustained bellicosity and frequently applied pressures. They also had a record of high union participation in most automobile plants. However, they could be distinguished from other Strategic groups by the extent of fractionated disputes, internal squabbling, multiple candidates for departmental stewardships, and inability to win high union office with any consistent frequency. Most importantly, they were distinguishable from other Strategic groups and resembled the Erratic groups insofar as they exhibited "contagion" in their concerted behavior, the activities of one group of trimmers serving to stimulate others. Thus many of their pressure tactics were not well planned, but tended toward the spontaneous and uncontrolled.

SUMMARY: THE STRATEGIC GROUPS

The most consistent concentration of high self-interest activity was found in a number of related groups we have called Strategic. We have given the largest number of examples under this heading because these groups were often the heart of the union as well as of the grievance activity in their respective plants. How management handled the difficult problems that arose in such departments was a prime factor in determining the existing climate of industrial relations. These departments were the real trouble spots, where management and union decisions were most likely to be vigorously and shrewdly challenged in the interests of improving the economic position of the employees concerned.

It is likely that the outsider would be shocked by the brashness and unceasing economic pressure of the Strategic groups. Such characteristics do not fit easily into the everyday concept of the grievance procedure—an appeal channel reserved for protesting inequitable management actions. These work groups use collective bargaining tactics, the whole range, in fact, to obtain benefits for themselves quite apart from any inequitable management action. In the process they come to set new standards for the plant as a whole for such matters as appropriate work loads, idle time, incentive earnings, and countless non-economic working conditions. As pace setters in the struggle to better themselves, they attract and require an unbelievably high proportion of management and union energies. Thus, identifying them and answering the question, "Why these groups rather than others?" becomes an important task for the administrator.

The groups we have called Strategic had a number of identifying characteristics in common:

1. Most of the jobs, with the exception of some of those in automobile manufacture, were individual operations; the jobs were not technologically interdependent as were most of those of the Erratic groups. In the case of automobile manufacture, particularly the body plants which were studied, there were no significant individual operations; all important work was done on the line. Although these production line groups were consistently centers of activity, as is characteristic of Strategic groups, they were also, on occasion, erratically demonstrative.

2. These jobs were better jobs than the majority of those in either of our two previous categories. In fact, they were close to the top in terms of worker preference among production jobs. However, it is important to note that in most instances they were not the best jobs in the plant. They were in a sense in the middle, between the relatively poor and the most desired positions.

3. The skills required by the jobs were often identified with personal-worker-judgment factors that made exact time standards difficult to apply. Even where tolerances were controlled by the settings of the machine, the operator sensed an important skill element because the finished product had been held to such close tolerances. Grieving over time and motion study standards was relatively easy.

4. The job was often one that was relatively important in the plant to management and the employees. There was a significant concentration of employees working at them, often senior employees who expected to make them "good" jobs, by pressure if necessary. Over the years they had looked forward to moving into such jobs and where the "goodness" of the job didn't meet their expectations, they sought to change the job, not their expectations. These posi-

tions were also, in fact if not in theory, the top of the promotional ladder for most of the men holding them. Promotions upward were few because the better jobs were limited in number and nearly always required apprenticeships or very good luck to obtain. Thus being committed to their present positions indefinitely, it was natural to expect concerted effort to make these positions the best ones.

The behavior characteristics of the Strategic groups are:

1. Continuous pressure.
2. Well planned and consistent grievance activity.
3. High degree of internal unity.
4. Sustained union participation.
5. Relatively good production records over the long run, for many of the groups, but not all.

Type iv: The Conservative Groups

Of all the groups we observed, the Conservative groups were the most stable, in the sense of being least likely to use concerted action without warning. Also, they were less likely to participate in union affairs. Management tended to be impressed with their overall record, while recognizing and accepting the fact that occasional well founded formal grievances do arise in such departments.

Their strength is insured by their economic position—a monopoly of critical, scarce skills. In those instances when they have sought and obtained top union leadership positions, they were known for their selfish approach to the leadership job. Their fellow union members commented: "On everything that comes up, they only ask one thing, 'How is it going to affect us? Are we going to get our share?' "

When they are not concerned with union politics, which is more typical than not of their group, they are also above the strains of the lesser skilled production worker. For example, in one company, the only group that had a paid lunch period was the automatic screw machine operators, the most skilled machining group in the plant. This exception to the general rule had been in existence for some years. The Conservatives often insisted on doing their own negotiating, so as not to be bound by the settlements of the majority. Some, in effect, have their own union; they are that self-sufficient.

The niche they have carved for themselves is often so satisfactory, in terms of their compensation and working conditions, that it is more common for management to have grievances against them, than for the men to have grievances against the management. It was not unusual to find the company attempting to negotiate a higher level of output with the group. This goal may be difficult to achieve, even when bonus systems and group strength guarantees that all additional effort will be reflected in higher earnings.

Summarizing, these kinds of groups are much more conservative in their grievance activities. On the surface at least, we saw little evidence of turmoil, trouble, or concerted activity. At some time or times in the past such a group had to exercise its strength; but once "proved," like the strength of any great power, it was accepted at face value by those whom it affected, until such time that they can match this power with greater force.

Representatives from these groups might be termed the senior statesmen of the plant negotiation machinery. Pyrotechnics are usually out of place, but when the occasion warrants it, a quick stoppage is always a possibility.

Because they are aware of their latent strength, they do not seem to demand the immediate service that is often demanded by the Erratic or Strategic groups. They can accept the time-consuming routine of the various channels and red tape of the grievance procedure without exploding with frustration. Less strong groups, when made to wait, are more likely to fear loss of the grievance unless they do "something"—and do it quickly. As others have observed, those with greater power can usually be more patient in waiting to secure their satisfaction.

For most of the men in the Conservative groups there is the probability that if the company does not provide satisfactory employment opportunities, there are an adequate number of jobs available requiring their specialization in the local labor market.

As the elite of the plant's labor force, they are self-conciously assured, successful, and relatively stable in their external relations with management as well as in their internal affairs. On occasion they exhibit ambivalence toward the union. They may experiment with leadership, and then leave active union affairs indefinitely, or they may even withdraw from the unified bargaining unit in favor of some craft union that will best represent them.

In our research we found a number of examples of such groups, other than the automatic screw machine operators. The *cutters* in the clothing industry immediately come to mind. Their economic strength and unity are unquestioned by the union or management. In the automobile industry, *general repairmen* and *dingmen*, who make final repairs on the metal body at the end of the assembly line, are indispensably skilled. In many ways they set their own price in terms of work standards. Their skills and position make prolonged struggles with management unnecessary. The same can be said for *pattern makers, die makers, and toolroom* personnel in industry generally. Where their skills are unquestioned, so is their power. (There are exceptional cases, of course, in which one or more of these groups exhibits "paranoid" tendencies. Then management can be assured that some unique factor is at work.)

Although most of these groups are characterized by individual non-interdependent operations and are concentrated geographically, some are what we would call "scatter groups." The members do not work together; rather they are assigned to work areas dominated by other occupational groups, for example, *inspectors, cranemen,* and *plant maintenance people.* It might be assumed that the locational factor would act as a block to unified action. In the short run this common-sense notion may have some validity. It takes time for a consensus to develop when workers see each other only sporadically during the work week. However, most such groups have an unbelievable array of channels through which common attitudes are cleared. Bill sees John who tells him how Harry and Joe feel. Bill then bumps into Henry and exchanges what Henry knows about Gus and Phil for what he knows about John, Harry and Joe.

A nice example of the triumph of the informal group over physical separation was furnished by the substation operators in two observed electrical utilities. As a group they are dispersed over the entire geographic area serviced by the company. However, they see each other at central dispatching stations and several work in groups at the larger stations. These individuals keep in touch with one another via intracompany telephones provided at each operating station. Thus, although widely dispersed, the operators have functioned as one of the most effective pressure groups in their respective companies. They have acted as a unit in selecting and electing top union officials and pressing for adjustments that increased their earnings substantially.[8]

At the lower rungs of this elite category, self-assured passivity is often costly in terms of group benefits. Here is where the indispensability factor is of lesser importance. Over a period of time, the more active groups among the less skilled production employees (the Strategics) may pull ahead, usually relatively, but on occasion in absolute monetary terms. This situation is a signal for some overdue

[8] I am indebted to Dr. George Strauss of the University of Buffalo for one of these cases.

internal reorganization of the union or the informal organization of the plant. For example, in one medium-sized manufacturing factory, plant inspectors had all but ignored the union from its inception. However, incentive bonuses for production workers and job reclassifications gradually diminished the inspectors' relative advantage over a period of years. Finally, the group decided to walk out in protest over their earnings and the rest of the plant followed them. Perhaps because of this success, they assumed a much more active role in the union. Although only a small percentage of the work force is classified as inspectors, their group now fills the two top positions in the local union and several additional executive board posts.[9]

If these inspectors respond like other work groups which classified in this same category, we would expect them to tire of union activity within the next few years and relinquish their posts to representatives of other departments. In turn, they gradually may suffer some deterioration in their relative standing on the plant benefit ladder. When this deterioration reaches some low point, they may be expected to resume aggressive activity.

Of course, they may not always be as successful as they were in this particular instance in winning control over union policies. Other departments then may be better situated to command votes and union recognition for their problems.

A number of similar examples can be furnished of maintenance and toolroom groups that have found themselves "behind." Usually the stimulus of some inequality is enough to galvanize them to action, and in the case of these groups, their inherent strength and cohesion gives some assurance that once aroused they will be successful in winning their objectives.

Some elite groups have waited "too long" to assert themselves. By the time they are roused to action, they have gained the reputation of being indifferent to the welfare of the rest of the plant by their unwillingness to participate in grievance activity. At such a time, the stage is set for a secession movement; typically there would be pressures from such a group for a craft unit of their own that would be distinct from the industrial union. As a result, manage-

[9] The reader may question how such a small group, originally inactive and having little in common with the great majority of production workers can gain such a position of ascendency in a plant-wide democratic ballot. Previous studies conducted by the author in collaboration with Professor Strauss show clearly that a small group of high-status employees can win elections consistently over less well paid opponents. The reasons for this are explored in some detail in our volume, Leonard Sayles and George Strauss, *The Local Union*, Harpers, New York 1953, pp. 143–150, 209.

ment might have to cope with the complexity of two or more unions in the shop with all the problems of invidious bargaining comparisons and of competition that this involves.

It was interesting to observe that in a number of instances the "steam" behind the secession movement quickly dissipated itself. The men who had been the most active protagonists were often caught in the backlash of a sudden change of heart on the part of their colleagues. Committed as they were to the formation of the new unit and a strong antimanagement policy, the leaders were often forced to resign from the company. Apparently, even in the formation of their own union, such groups lack persistence and consistency born of the major disequilibrium that seems to be characteristic of the Strategic groups.

Thus, those Conservative work groups which are not really so indispensable as some of their colleagues, or in as short supply, may periodically have to take up the cudgels of grievance activity. When they do so, their activities are more moderate, and more short-lived than those exhibited by the Strategic groups.

Actually, in many cases we find a cycle:

Passivity—gradual rise in the feeling of being left out.

Activity—success in improving relative position.

Satisfaction with new relative position.

Passivity—and so on around the cycle.

For the most part, however, the Conservative groups are peaceful and well adjusted; their problems are solved by relatively frictionless adjustments, not by pressure tactics. Through their leadership they make demands on management both in and out of the formal grievance channels, and management responds favorably.

SUMMARY: THE CONSERVATIVE GROUPS

For the most part these were groups located at the top rungs of both the promotional and status ladders of the plant. They were self-assured and successful, and they only went into action when some existing benefit was threatened or when they found themselves "behind the parade"—due to the ceaseless pressures of some less well endowed (and therefore less "worthy") work area.

Most of their work involves individual operations, but on occasion several employees will work together in a repair or maintenance crew. Common also is a wide distribution of their members throughout the plant—what we have called scatter groups.

Behavior characteristics of conservative groups are:

1. Restrained pressure for highly specific objectives.
2. Moderate internal unity and self-assurance.
3. Activity—inactivity cycles in terms of union activities and the plant grievance procedure.

SUMMARY

We have observed that in looking at the long-run behavior of a large number of industrial work groups, certain categories or types emerge. That is, it has been possible to identify four rather specific patterns of action and reaction which these work groups follow in their relations to management and the union. We have called these patterns: (1) Apathetic. (2) Erratic. (3) Strategic. (4) Conservative.

Their respective features are summarized on the following diagram.

SUMMARY OF WORK GROUP DIFFERENCES

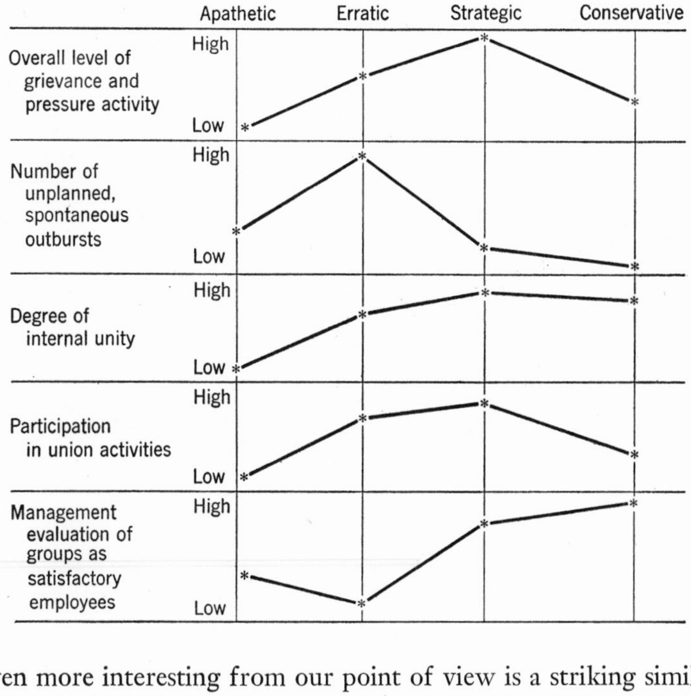

Apathetic Erratic Strategic Conservative

Overall level of grievance and pressure activity — High / Low

Number of unplanned, spontaneous outbursts — High / Low

Degree of internal unity — High / Low

Participation in union activities — High / Low

Management evaluation of groups as satisfactory employees — High / Low

Even more interesting from our point of view is a striking similarity in technological characteristics among groups that behave similarly. In the several plants from which we were able to obtain descriptions, wire drawers consistently acted like a Strategic group regardless of the company in which they were located, as did welders, grinders, pressers, etc., behave in a predictable fashion. The trimmers and metal finishers had industry-wide reputations for their activities. Drill press operators and similar workers were consistently Apathetic. Where we have described certain unique operations like the engine block chippers, the tub polishers, and the strippers, it was for the purpose of illustrating the common technological similarities that exist in the face of the more obvious differences in the nature of the work performed.

It is the function of the next chapter to clarify these technological similarities that lie behind the distinctive patterns of work group behavior. Our raw material will be the description of what work they do and how the work is performed. Even when we can identify certain characteristics the Apathetic groups have in common, or similarities among the Strategic groups, we must still answer the question of why these characteristics should lead to a particular pattern of in-plant behavior. In attempting to answer this question we must rely to a considerable degree on inference from the data in hand.

chapter 3

Explaining work group differences

In the previous chapter we attempted to describe four distinct patterns of work group behavior, to which we appended the names: Apathetic, Erratic, Strategic, and Conservative. While it is useful to be able to identify or classify relatively durable reaction patterns on the part of work groups, the value of this type of analysis is increased substantially if it can be shown that behavior differences are grounded in other differences among these worker aggregations. The exploration of these other differences is the subject of this chapter.

Persistent, sustained, and intelligently contrived grievance and other pressure activity must require an unusual degree of internal group strength. Aside from the risks involved of losing the friendship of management and/or union representatives, the members must often endure substantial deprivation in the way of earnings and peace of mind. Except in the most unified of groups, differences of opinion concerning both objectives and tactics will dissipate that most essential ingredient of any frontal attack—absolute solidity of agreement among the members.

Not only is a high degree of cohesiveness required, but the interest group must be sufficiently inclusive to present management and the union with the undeniable conclusion that the matter in question is of supreme importance to everyone involved. If the matter involves the widget handlers, every widget handler, or nearly every one, needs to be a part of the protest group.

Further, there is an important element of self-control involved. The group that demands immediate satisfaction, that protests almost spontaneously and expects relief simultaneously, is often being unrealistic in terms of the operations of the grievance procedure. Its activities may impede rather than facilitate the efforts of its leaders.

We believe that a group's behavior in the plant is a product of its *inherent ability to function in a certain way*. Its behavior over time, particularly its reaction to changes introduced by management, and its perceptions of inequity are predictable, because the range of alternative means of reacting is severely limited.

These capabilities or predetermining characteristics are the focus of our interest here. Initially we shall be exploring variables relating to the status of the work: the degree of skill required and its relative remuneration, the size of the job and its expendability, the ease and accuracy with which management can set production standards, the repetitiveness of the work, the proximity of employees to one another, their sex, and the hours of work.

Our observations indicate that the internal structuring of the work operations, which we shall examine next, also affect significantly the behavior characteristics of a group. That is, the relation between members prescribed by the flow of work process are a critical variable shaping the internal social system of the group. Here we shall explore the difference between work operations that involve interdependence among employees (where the efforts of one are dependent on the efforts of a colleague), and the jobs that permit an employee to complete his task essentially independently, without continuous interaction with fellow employees.

Again, our objective in all of this is to relate the behavior of work groups to various explanatory factors. Because of the common features that exist in the technological organization of work, we think a share of the answer to industrial relations problems lies in these factors.

A. Intergroup Factors Affecting Collective Behavior

The first set of possible causal factors that we want to explore is related to the status of the work itself, in relation to other jobs and other work groups in the organization. This section explores the effect on group behavior of the following variables of intergroup comparison.

Position on the promotional ladder
Size of the work group
Relative internal homogeneity
Essentialness of their function
Work standards involving judgment
Repetitiveness of the task
Compactness (of the work area)
Sex differences
Hours of work

POSITION ON THE PROMOTIONAL LADDER

The relative ranking of the job performed by the members of the work group (in comparison to other jobs in the organization) seems highly important in explaining certain aspects of their grievance behavior. At the very extremes of the job ladder the evidence is rather simple and easy to assess. Work groups at the bottom of the job ladder and those at the very top of the in-plant structure tend to show less concerted activity than those in the middle ranges. The reasons for this similarity of behavior are not identical, however, nor is the behavior itself, on closer examination.

An individual employee's willingness to support a given interest group in its efforts to improve the benefits shared by the group or to defend some vested interest depends, to some extent at least, on his commitment to his present job. The activities just referred to involve risks, extending to the very real threat of discharge for participating in an unpopular work interruption. When an employee sees his present job as a temporary way station to a promotion or a position outside the plant, participation in such campaigns would hardly be worthwhile, except in those instances when he is seeking an emotional scapegoat—a chance to explode, rather than a rational objective.

For the non-Erratic groups, therefore, one finds self-interest activity concentrated in departments where the workers have some accumulated seniority and the likelihood of relatively long tenure in their present positions. Our own studies of grievance behavior confirm the overrepresentation of the more prestigeful members of the plant community.[1] Recently an investigator of unofficial strikes in

[1] Leonard Sayles and George Strauss, *The Local Union*, Harpers, New York, 1953, p. 68.

the coal mining industry in Great Britain found that the highest paid production workers (taking into account incentive earnings) contributed most of the stoppages and the lowest paid workers the least, with the craft workers presumably falling somewhere in the middle.[2]

As Chinoy notes in his study of a large automobile plant, those who expect to leave the plant are concentrated in the younger age-seniority bracket.[3] Given strong emphasis on hiring at the bottom and on promotion from within, in production jobs at least, we would find these men on the poorer paying, less skilled, less prestigeful jobs. Also, the younger age-seniority brackets produce somewhat more than their share of workers who are still hopeful of promotion into management, another reason for caution in their behavior. Furthermore, these younger men lack the experience—they "don't know the ropes"—that facilitates adept handling of their own grievances. High turnover in such jobs, both as a result of promotions and quitting, militates against strong, self-sufficient groups.

This type of job has another influence on the incidence of concerted attempts by the incumbents to improve their status. The less desirable occupations have a greater proportion of men who are marking time, who are waiting to accumulate enough seniority to get a good job. There is something incongruous, and inappropriate, about taking steps to improve a job that everyone in the plant assumes is a poor job. In the automobile industry again, as Chinoy observes, assembly line work is considered to be almost at the bottom of the preference hierarchy.[4] Few think of it as a good job, or for that matter, expect it to be. Most of the persons in this type of work hope to leave it as soon as a "break" or seniority makes it possible. Except for protests directed toward management changes that threaten to make it a "worse job," and occasional explosions that have little direction, we do not find self-improvement activities in such work groups.

One union leader with long experience in the automobile plants contrasted two types of assembly operations, neither of which produces many of the long-run strategic actions characteristic of departments having better jobs.

[2] George B. Baldwin, *Beyond Nationalization: The Labor Problems of British Coal,* Harvard University Press, Cambridge, 1955, pp. 86–87.

[3] Eli Chinoy, *Automobile Workers and the American Dream,* Random House, New York, 1955, pp. 87–88.

[4] *Ibid.,* p. 76. It should be noted that here and in the material to follow the discussion refers to the unskilled assembler jobs and not the more skilled clusters that exist in the automobile plants we have described previously, such as metal finishers, etc.

The body shop is the kind of place where you would get tired if you just stood around and watched—it's in the terrific pace of the work, the noise and the dirt and smoke and heat. This is where you get all the explosions—the wildcats. But the motor line is different; it's repetitive and monotonous work—the screwing on of the same few bolts every day. This is the kind of department where you hear about the man who has had a perfect work record for 26 years, never having protested or participated in a strike, no grievances, but one day he suddenly gets up and socks the foreman.

On the other hand, the undesirable conditions of the work do give rise to much personal dissatisfaction which may be expressed in the form of petty complaints.

Jobs at the very bottom or close to the very bottom of the promotional ladder may also include a number of employees who have given up any notions of self-improvement. Lacking any desire for mobility, and avoiding promotion and increased responsibility, they are equally reluctant to make the effort required to improve their present jobs. This self-selection process limits the types of jobs in which we would expect to find active, aggressive, self-seeking employees.

On the other side, for the one who is on top, not only is there less to struggle for, but also, management, if its expressed attitudes are any guide to its behavior, is more likely to concede matters at issue. We consistently heard that highly paid occupational groups had more "reasonable," "intelligent," "worthwhile," "well-founded" grievances. Even assuming that many of these evaluations are invalid, such opinions cannot help influencing management reaction to their grievances. For a case originating in a low status department, the executive frequently begins with the preconception, "This is undoubtedly another foolish grievance with no basis in fact." In contrast, in a high status department, the first impression is often, "There must be something to this if they are raising a complaint." Concerted activity may be less necessary in the latter instance. Significantly, work groups appear to be quite sensitive in assessing management "class bias," even when it is disguised in the legalism of the grievance procedure.

Some of the highest-paying jobs have a heavy proportion of men nearing retirement and a company pension. Even with the union acting as a watchdog, they are reluctant to take an extra chance of exposing themselves to some penalty that could lead to discharge. Furthermore, these men, being older in most instances, have less need for additional income, having finished paying for homes and the education of children.

Some substantial degree of in-plant prestige is probably essential for high activity. As we have shown in our study of the internal life of the local union, union members are more likely to select relatively high status candidates for union positions; there is something that inspires confidence in the incumbent of a relatively high-paying job.[5] Similar studies have shown that higher status persons themselves have more confidence in their political abilities and are more likely to express them.

> It has often been observed that participation in national politics varies with position in the society; it may similarly be suggested that the higher the status of the worker, the more likely he is to claim a right in decision making. . . .[6]

This claim is demonstrated by the willingness to participate actively in the grievance procedure, and the formulation of demands in negotiations, because these demands are the basic union decisions which affect group welfare.

Apparently, the higher status groups also demonstrate greater internal solidarity. Internal bickerings and open battles are far more limited in such work groups. Several explanations are possible. The easiest, which often is stated by supervisors, is that the "kind of worker" differs, and that "In the better jobs you get better people."

In fact, class differences may be of some modest significance in the prevalence of actual open aggression. Fighting may be more acceptable among the less privileged socio-economic groups, and insofar as there could be some slight correlation between the socio-economic level of the neighborhood from which the employee comes and the job level he attains in the plant, we would expect less emphasis on interpersonal struggle in higher skilled, higher paid occupational groups. This factor may also carry over into the worker-management area. If a grievance or a strike is perceived as a type of fighting, it will not be resorted to readily by groups which are not inclined to displays of aggression. It should be underlined that these ideas are highly speculative.

It will be recalled that on jobs where the least skill is required and the wages are lowest we have noted that grievances, and concerted activity of all sorts are almost non-existent. However, interpersonal squabbling is frequent and at this level the correlation may be a better one.

[5] Sayles and Strauss, *op. cit.,* p. 150.

[6] S. M. Lipset, "The Political Process in Trade Unions: A Theoretical Statement," in M. Berger, T. Abel, and C. Page, *Freedom and Control in Modern Society,* Van Nostrand, New York, 1954, p. 117.

Another factor affecting the degree of concerted activity demonstrated by a group may be the nature of the members' work itself. Jobs with prestige commonly provide more diversified, challenging work. Put simply, the persons on these jobs may be better satisfied and thus less inclined to demonstrate against management and/or the union. However, this hypothesis is not borne out by the data. Surprisingly, there is no evidence in our study that groups performing interesting work are less aggressive than groups performing routine, boring tasks.[7]

Status in the Automobile Industry. The automobile industry provides some interesting examples of closely related work groups whose patterns of behavior are quite distinctive. Although we have discussed these in the previous chapter let us review their characteristics, concentrating on the status variable.

The following are closely related occupational groups which fall in a promotional sequence: diskers, wet sanders, metal finishers, and dingmen. All are working in small groups, and their jobs are somewhat similar—eliminating various imperfections in the metal surface of the automobile body. However, there is substantial variation in the "concerted-interest-behavior" records of the four groups in the plants we surveyed.

A. Disking is primarily a roughing operation. It precedes the other operations and is considered dangerous, as well as noisy and unpleasant. The work area is fully enclosed and thus partly isolated from the remainder of the plant. It is assumed that little skill is required to utilize the power tools involved, and management often has difficulty in finding men to take the job. When the work force is decreased, although the operation is included in the promotional ladder, men are not required to demote into this job. Although the working conditions are distinctly unpleasant (masks are required to protect men's lungs from the metal dust produced), grievances are not prevalent. In fact, there is a minimum of self-interest activity.

B. The next step above disking in terms of job status is *wet sanding.* Less unpleasant than disking, but still considered a poor job because of the physical effort involved and the necessity for keeping one's hands immersed in water (required by the sanding materials used), wet sand is one of the plant hot spots. The men work as a compact team on automobile bodies as they proceed from the line. Some judgment and skill are required, but it is mostly a question of brawn. Little disturbing factors cause major explosions.

[7] This statement will be discussed in more detail in a later section, titled *Repetitiveness of the Task*, p. 67.

C. The *metal finishers* are really at the top of the promotional ladder. Although only a few cents per hour separate them from the previous two groups, they are considered fairly skilled for automobile production workers. Substantial judgment is required and working conditions are good compared to those in the lower-rated jobs. These men are the legalistic, steady-grievance processors, always attempting to get their work standards adjusted, often by means of a carefully timed slowdown.

D. Very few metal finishers become *dingmen.* They are the real artists of the body shop, and only a small number are required on any line. They work in scattered locations, often off the line, doing the final touch-up work on slight blemishes that were missed or created at earlier stages. Good dingmen are hard to find; many managers insist they are "born, not made." Rarely does one hear of any need for force on the part of dingmen. Management readily makes adjustments to meet their problems.

As can be observed, with increased earnings and skill (judgment) the behavior pattern shifts from Apathetic to Conservative.

Job	Behavior Category	Work Description
Disking	Apathetic	Used in automobile industry. Dirty, dangerous work, utilizing power sanding. The first roughing stage for which primarily muscle, not skill, is required.
Wet Sanding	Erratic	Also has major physical component, but easier than disking. Closeness to final finish means some judgment and skill required, but mostly brawn.
Metal Polishers and Finishers	Strategic	Although a semiskilled production job, sufficient judgment is required so that standards tend to be loose. Considered quite skilled, one of best production jobs of large group.
Dingmen	Conservative	In many ways a craft, although not formally designated as such. Management considers almost irreplaceable. Only a small number employed.

The Middle Range. While prestige factors tend to disqualify groups at the extremes of the scale from high concerted activity, they serve to motivate those groups which are in the middle range of the status ladder of the plant. Such groups do not have jobs which are obviously and inevitably undesirable, nor do they occupy positions which are manifestly the most superior available. They are neither the most discriminated against nor catered to. The groups in the middle range of jobs in the factory are most likely to strive to improve their situations in terms of job classification, incentive rates, perquisites, and all the rest. They are the ones who are not content with management evaluations of the relative worth of their positions.

Many of the jobs in this middle class are not well defined by the local labor market. Typically, many skilled jobs at the top of promotional ladders and unskilled jobs at the very bottom are somewhat similar from firm to firm. They are also "hiring" jobs, insofar as a firm tends to hire directly into these positions, while the middle jobs tend to be steps on an internal promotional ladder. As a result, what are fair and equitable wage rates, in terms of the "going rate" in the community, tend to be substantially more ambiguous for the middle range of occupations.[8] For the other jobs the levels of expectation of the employees are more realistic perhaps, based as they are on well-defined job rates in the labor market. With regard to the middle range jobs, however, there is always one factor or another for incumbents to grasp which seems to justify their being worth more in the scale of plant values than their currently stated position reflects. There is, we would say, enough ambiguity of status to make efforts at wage or status improvement seem reasonable.

Tool sharpeners are *almost* the equivalent of cutter grinders. Hand screw machine operators are *almost* as skilled as automatic screw machine operators. Wire drawers' jobs are *almost* the best in the various steel plants in which we observed them, as are trimmers in automobile body shops. Some metal finishing is *almost* a craftsman's art. Production grinders are *almost* as skilled as tool grinders; their tolerances are nearly as close. These are the kind of jobs which fit into the middle range.[9]

[8] Cf. Robert L. Raimon, "The Indeterminateness of Wages of Semiskilled Workers," *Industrial and Labor Relations Review,* VI, 1953, pp. 180–194.

[9] A union official called attention to another interesting example of a middle group being the most active. On the basis of his observation, in the maritime trades—when the entire vessel is organized by the same union, the engine room personnel are the most vigorous in pursuing their objectives. They rank in prestige above the employees in the galley, but below the men who work on the deck, the highest prestige group among the non-officer groups on the ship.

Sometimes the parallel is striking. In the fabrication of steel into metal parts, the men who regrind the cutting edges of the tools, thinking themselves far above the production machinist, and the equivalent of the broadly skilled toolroom personnel, were a continuous source of grievances. In basic steel, we found the comparable group exhibited identical behavior. These were *roll grinders* who reground the surfaces of the rolls used in rolling steel. They too claimed skills comparable to the elite, all-around toolmaker, but were denied this status by management who calculated their job classification in production terms.

In these jobs we find men who are committed to a given occupation for an extended period. The jobs tend to be at the top of a particular promotional ladder, and further advancement is unlikely in the foreseeable future. It has been observed that, over time, employees are likely to grow more dissatisfied as it becomes evident that their expectations for getting ahead will not be satisfied. In a sense, seniority breeds discontent.[10]

AN ILLUSTRATIVE CASE: THE HAND SCREW MACHINE DEPARTMENT—A MIDDLE-CLASS DEPARTMENT

A closer look at one department which fits into this category may clarify the meaning of "ambiguity of status." To be sure, this is an extreme case in the degree of contrast between expectations and reality as regards job importance, but it illustrates the dynamics of the problem.

The group included about twenty-five men, each assigned to a single machine. Their operation requires substantial skill, in some ways approximately a toolroom skill, but hand screw machine jobs are still considered production machinist's work. This unit comprised one of the largest groupings of identical machines in the plant. Although there were serious dissatisfactions over rates, it was the highest-paid production job in the plant.

Few of the employees in the department expected to rise above their present job, and the general attitude was stated by one of them: "You've got to be a toolmaker or an engineer to make assistant foreman, and you've got to be crazy to want to be a job setter, with all his headaches, for a few more pennies an hour."

The management believes the department is a hotbed for malcontents, that somehow the worst elements in the shop have gravitated there, and further, that it is producing a steady stream of "ill-founded grievances." Management also is under the impression that the men

[10] Cf. Daniel Katz, "Survey Research Center: An Overview of the Human Relations Program," in *Groups, Leadership and Men,* edited by H. Guetzkow, Carnegie Press, Pittsburgh, 1951, pp. 77–78.

have a highly inflated conception of the skill necessary to perform their jobs: "The skill is built into the machines, not the men."

"We can break in men in six months and then they can do as well as any man in the department. The machine does all the work—they just put in the pieces and take them out, and they don't really hold those close tolerances they are always talking about. Why the multiple drill press is just as skilled work as theirs!"

This kind of appraisal is in sharp contrast to the men's image of their work. They are convinced that their jobs are substantially more skilled than the management recognizes:

"A friend of mine owns his own job shop; he didn't believe me when I told him the tolerances we keep! Over in X Company they refused a contract to do this kind of work; they claimed they couldn't do it at production rates."

"Everyone you tell that you are working to 3/10ths limits with this equipment says it is impossible."

"In the old days we used to earn 10 cents more an hour than the men in the toolroom—that's how skilled our work is—and other men in the shop would be getting less than half of what we would be earning an hour."

"During the war when toolmakers were scarce they raised them up. We've never been able to gain back what we lost then. Even now we can run jobs the toolroom can't."

"Our type of work shouldn't be on incentive—it's the quality that counts."

But self-doubts have crept in. Not only is management's present evaluation unfavorable (witness the small differential separating the wages of this group and those of unskilled groups), but their fellow workers do not support them.

"Want these jobs? No one. People think we're crazy to do this kind of work for the money we get."

"Even the guys on trucks won't transfer in here and they've got the lowest rates in the plant."

"And it's dirty too; you're always working in oil and lots of people get skin diseases."

"At least half the men would leave if they had the chance. Some are even studying electronics, hoping to better themselves while others will take any job they can get outside of the department."

More threatening yet to their beliefs is the fact that the men recognize defections in their own ranks. It was believed that large numbers of men have been seeking transfers, even to lower paying jobs, and men who were demoted during a cutback in employment refuse to return to the department.

A new rumor was started, based on the combination of two attitudes: that management doesn't "like" the department any longer and that the job is no longer popular.

"Now if you make a mistake in some other department they send you here as a penalty and you can't transfer out."

This situation is a comedown for a group that lays claim to have been earning "more than the toolroom in the old days."

The level of tension runs high in the department. The men blame it on "the machine limits we have to keep on defense jobs." Some stated that conditions are so bad "the men take it out on their wives." We would speculate that the ambiguity concerning the importance of their job is also a contributing factor.

Even with these self-doubts brought on by unfavorable comparisons with other departments, fears concerning management's evaluation, the attitudes of other groups toward them, and the recognition that many of their own group desire a transfer elsewhere, a certain level of assurance remains. This keeps the group intact. Nearly every one interviewed was convinced that the men in the department "were closer together than any group I have known." The interviewees attributed this closeness to the "kind of men the job attracted," but more importantly:

"What holds our group together is the fact that we have the highest base rate of any production job in the plant."

Their unity was demonstrated in many ways. During a recent department strike "not a man wanted to stay in." Certainly this closeness was reassuring to them—they all felt the same way about their jobs and their demands. In addition the men were able to solve by themselves some difficult seniority problems that, in other work groups, had led to internal bickerings. They also evolved their own emergency fund to which everyone contributed (the fund would pay benefits to the members struck by catastrophe).

The men have rationalized their inability to obtain earnings commensurate with their opinions of the value of their job. In part, they believe, their plight has resulted from unfriendly, unsympathetic supervision (men who have a toolroom background, who are not from their own group). Then they refer to the wartime shortage of toolmakers which changed the relative earnings in the plant. But most consistently they blame their difficulty on another external factor: the failure of management to develop efficient methods of supervision. As one "shop lawyer" in the group described the problem:

"There is just too much buck passing for the mistakes that are made. The engineers and production control people are too inefficient, and there is too much non-production help running around, like stock chasers. Whenever production is delayed we have to make up the loss —in fact we pay for it. The whole thing boils down to the fact that the company isn't making enough money. Someone has to pay the wages for all these people who don't produce anything and obviously it has to be us.

Thus they have the opinion, not that there is any lack of abilities or skill among hand screw machine operators, but that upper management has been blinded by inadequate lower supervision and the lack of adequate profits. They think that they would get paid more if only these *external forces* would change.

So this was the unusual combination of attitudes:

"We're the best production group in terms of the quality and skill of the work we do, even if others don't recognize it. Somehow we have got to convince management that we are that skilled."

One of the ways these men chose to obtain their objectives was to engage in a wildcat strike. They demanded higher earnings among other things. But the sudden walkout was a miserable failure. They did not get the support they had expected from other departments, and the management did not concede any of the points at issue.

"We didn't gain a thing from the strike; that's all there is to it. All we did was lose a few days' pay. I can assure you, it won't happen again this way. We just came back to the same conditions that we had when we walked out."

In pursuing some of the interviews it was apparent that they did not come back "to the same conditions that we had when we walked out." They had discovered what some of the other men thought of them:

"Over in the toolroom, I heard they laughed at us when we had our strike; they said the company ought to fire the whole lot of us!"

They obtained ridicule, not support, and were more aware than ever that they were perceived as "troublemakes," "hotheads," and "radicals" by the management. And all of these opinions conflicted with their conception of the prestige of their job.

This ambivalence of attitude was dramatically expressed by one employee:

"It isn't good for the men or for the company that we are known as a group of radicals. . . . yet I guess some of the men are getting so they don't care any more. I know I don't care any longer what higher supervision thinks of me."

The events described above form a typical pattern in such departments, where the employees' unsuccessful efforts to gain recognition further aggravate their status problem in the plant community. Because the work does have many of the attributes of an important job —high pay, close tolerances, responsibility—these men continue to try to improve their status.

Thus a vicious cycle is established: (1) doubts concerning the importance of the job; (2) efforts to gain further recognition; (3) new evidence for feeling the job is not "appreciated," resulting from these efforts; (4) renewed efforts to raise their status and that of their jobs by means of new grievances and pressure tactics.

It is important to note that a group which lacks basic structural unity, partly founded on the actual status of the job, would not have gotten itself into this dilemma. (Other elements which enabled the group in our illustration to wage a long-run campaign will be discussed in the sections to follow.) Their initial failures more likely would have quelled any further demonstrations; nor would the reactions of others, particularly of management in terms of "you are troublemakers," have been so resented. Men who feel their work is important and skilled find it difficult to think of themselves as hotheads. They feel themselves to be highly responsible, not irresponsible. Furthermore, as we indicated, the department under discussion was highly cohesive.

It bears repeating that the core of the problem was a range of uncertainty concerning the absolute value of the job. It did have elements of high skill and importance, but it also had elements of being just another production job, like milling and drilling and all the rest. Historically there were factors which caused the men to see the importance of their job. There had been unusually high overtime earnings for a relatively long period, when this was a bottleneck operation. It is doubtful that the wages earned by these men were ever more than toolroom rates, but what is important is that the men believed that such a condition once existed. This then was one of those "in-the-middle" jobs.

Until the whole range of factors that contribute to the workers' evaluation of their job and their status comes into alignment—earnings, absolute differentials between jobs, skill levels, opinions of other workers, of management, and of fellow workers—this department is likely to be the source of many plant problems. The basic instabilities will create situation after situation, and the men have that high degree of unity which will enable them to convert dissatisfaction into active opposition.

There is a certain ordering of events that makes the eventual explosions seem almost inevitable. The expectations of the employees as to the relative worth and importance of the job are greater than can be satisfied. The results are self-sustaining, self-feeding grievances.

We have seen similar behavior among technicians in manufacturing plants, even though the job skills employed were of quite a different kind. In one company in particular there were large numbers of these employees scattered through both production and staff departments. Lacking the educational requirements as well as the job descriptions that would qualify them for the title of "engineer," they grew increasingly dissatisfied. After a period an engineers' club was formed in the company which met weekly, ostensibly to foster the social and intellectual interests of all of the company's engineers. However, it soon became apparent that the club was not anxious to admit employees already holding the title of engineer. As the club became more exclusive, the members began to concentrate their activities on pressuring management to upgrade many of the technicians' jobs to the status of engineers' jobs. Here again was an example of an "in-the-middle" group, one that *almost* qualified for the top rung of the prestige ladder (in this case the engineer rating), assuming the role of a Strategic group. There were a substantial number of men in this position, and concerted interest behavior evolved quite naturally, although union activities, if identified as such, would have been an anathema to the group.

In summary, the effect of the position on the promotional ladder on work group behavior is as follows:

The status of the work done by a group is believed to be an important factor affecting its pattern of behavior. It affects the attitude of the members toward each other and toward their group. Self-confidence, even self-righteousness, is a product of recognized value. Furthermore, as researchers on small groups have observed, individual conformity to group norms and goals, so essential for concerted action, is easier to obtain when the members are highly attracted to the jobs, as they are more likely to be on skilled and well-paying jobs.[11]

In contrast, low prestige jobs are likely to contain larger than proportionate shares of young newcomers, low seniority employees, persons marking time until seniority brings them promotions, unambitious individuals, and workers who intend to remain only until they can find better jobs. Employees of these types do not exert vigorous pressure for the improvement of their working conditions.

We have suggested that the highest prestige groups in the plant are so favored in their various endowments that they are less likely to exhibit open pressure tactics; the least favored are incapacitated for such tactics.

Thus overt concerted interest behavior tends to be more concentrated in the "upper middle groups," many of which fall into our description of Erratic and Strategic behavior patterns. These are also the groups which are likely to have ambiguous standards of employee evaluation and to contain the greatest number of dissatisfied employees. Typically, promotions from these groups are rare because the openings in the more skilled groups are likely to be filled by ap-

[11] Cf. Leon Festinger, "Informal Communication in Small Groups," in *Groups, Leadership and Men*, edited by H. Guetzkow, Carnegie Press, Pittsburgh, 1951, pp. 35 ff.

prenticeships or by the hiring of skilled persons directly from the community labor market.

The prestige given a group by its work is likely to influence both management and union in their handling of grievances as well. Important groups are supposed to have important cases. The groups below the very top of the promotional ladder find their problems taken somewhat more lightly, and they probably have to exert more pressure to get acceptable adjustments of their complaints. Aggressiveness becomes essential for the purpose of upbuilding and maintaining status.

SIZE OF THE WORK GROUP

It would seem reasonable that relative size might also be a variable affecting a work group's propensity to engage in various kinds of aggressive activity. However, the "reasonable" hypotheses extend in two quite opposing directions. Research conducted by the group dynamics school and recently confirmed by the Survey Research Center suggests that group cohesiveness (defined as the *attractiveness* of the group to its members) is inversely correlated with size.[12] Cohesion in these terms is more characteristic of small than large groups. Since we expect that the cohesiveness of the group affects its ability to conduct external pressure campaigns, small groups might be expected to be vigorous and successful in such endeavors.

Another reason for expecting small groups to be inclined toward concerted activity is the experience of craft groups. Labor economists have observed that a small craft group, whose wages represent a relatively small percentage of the total labor cost of the enterprise, is in an obviously stronger position to secure wage concessions than are larger groups or the entire work force of a plant. The employer will more willingly concede to a small group, particularly when their labor is essential and their skills difficult to replace, than to a large group whose total wages are a greater proportion of the total payroll.

On the other hand, the total amount of influence a group has in the union and in the eyes of management may be positively related to size. In the eyes of most "old hands," the worker's success in pressing a grievance is directly related to the number of people willing to claim it with him as an inequity. "The louder you can shout, the more

[12] Stanley Seashore, *Group Cohesiveness in the Individual Work Group,* Institute for Social Research, Ann Arbor, 1954, p. 99.

likely they will hear you and listen to you." With these considerations in mind, size would be a positive advantage.[13]

Another effect of size (assuming that we are interested in assessing the likelihood of effective concerted action on the part of work groups) is the increased probability afforded to the development of adequate leadership. Although we shall deal with leadership at some length later, here we are merely pointing to the probability factor. Particularly for groups lacking a membership with educational and leadership experience, size can increase the chances that one or two members will develop the skills which are indispensable to the group process.

Of course group size may also contribute to the pool of dissatisfaction which gets expressed in concerted action. It has been observed that low morale (in terms of attitude toward management and the job) is associated with large concentrations of employees doing similar tasks.[14] In one of the large automobile companies, departments containing large concentrations of draftsmen were referred to as "Siberia." The men themselves admitted that grievances festered more readily under these conditions, as compared to areas where only a few draftsmen worked. Presumably there is less sense of job satisfaction in large social groups.

In general, our data tend to support the hypothesis that greater size is associated with more concerted activity. Particularly in the case of Strategic groups, those most active in pressing for benefits appeared to be relatively large concentrations of employees (for the given plant or division). The importance of size is seen most clearly in plants where there are a number of distinct work groups with similar internal structures at approximately the same level of skill and earnings.

For example, in a large carton manufacturing plant, there were approximately a half dozen work groups, corresponding to the various operations through which the paperboard passed while being converted into finished carton. All the jobs were similar, requiring almost equal skill and paying similar rates. However, about 50 per cent more persons operated one type of machine than the number which

[13] Chandler notes that the pressers in her sample of clothing plants were only a real power where they had twelve or fifteen in the group. Just two or three pressers in a department precluded any effective power. Margaret Chandler, *Labor-Management Relations in Illini City, Case Study 3: Garment Manufacture*, University of Illinois, Institute of Labor and Industrial Relations, Champaign, Ill., 1953, p. 457.

[14] Cf. Mason Haire, *Psychology in Industry*, McGraw Hill Book Co., New York, 1956, pp. 28–29.

operated any other type. This group, the largest in the plant, was also the most active in pressing grievances. The members regularly elected one of their number as union representative for the division and their unit served as the "pattern setter" for the division.

In many instances the interest groups whose behavior was studied in this survey numbered 100 or more employees. A typical group was equivalent to 3 to 5 per cent of the total plant labor force.

Notable exceptions were provided by a number of small groups we called "island groups." Typically, the members of each of these were located physically in the center of another work group that was doing a different kind of work. For example, within some of the long assembly lines there were small groups (no more than twelve workers) of testers or adjusters. These groups seemed to be more conscious of their prerogatives and needs than similar occupational groups that were not completely surrounded by large numbers of employees engaged in very different types of work. It is worth noting that the surrounding workers usually lacked any single strong occupational identification.

Aside from such exceptions, continuous and successful interest group activity, characteristic of Strategic groups, seemed to have as a prerequisite a number of adherents that was reasonably large in relation to the total plant working force. This prerequisite was not true, however, of Erratic or Conservative groups. The explosiveness of the Erratic units would often be restricted to a small primary group, and many of the Conservative groups were the economist's small craft enclaves whose strength was, in part, a function of their small size.

Size then was not quite the clear-cut factor one would like it to be, but there was evidence that it was frequently associated with concerted activity.

INTERNAL HOMOGENEITY

Size, however, had a potent effect when it was combined with homogeneity. In previous sections we have often referred to the effect of similar interests among group members on group strength and activity. Generally speaking, we found that adjacently located employees who operated different kinds of machines or performed different tasks were not prone to associate in a pressure group to attain mutual goals. They did not have enough in common. These were frequently the Apathetic groups.

What seemed essential for verbalizing complaints and uniting people to "right them" was some reinforcement or *resonance* factor. Where this reverberation was provided by people having identical experiences, each one could hear his own grievances repeated and magnified. Each man who told his mates of a job problem found that they too shared it. With sympathetic repetition the problem grew in importance.

The individual standing alone is unlikely to risk too many demands. He knows that grievers are identified by both union and management as troublemakers.[15] But a group of like-minded employees may convince one another, not only that something *should* be done, but more importantly, that it *can* be done! [16]

Our hypothesis then is that, other things being equal, the greater the number of workers affected by some aspect of the work environment the more likely they will act in common against the problem.

Below, three observers of industry comment from completely different points of view on this resonance factor. Each one, generalizing from distinctive data, concludes that homogeneity contributes to concerted group behavior because any individual's feelings are multiplied in an environment of like-minded fellows.

> . . . The fewer differences there are in work-group status (and pay) consistent with . . . opportunities for promotion, the more likely is the internal structure of a group to stabilize itself and the more likely are its members to accept internal leadership.[17]

> A respectable body of management theory encourages the setting up of kindred activities, wherever possible, as semi-dependent units on the assumption, apparently, that separation and specialization will permit better supervision, make possible smoother scheduling, and generally improve efficiency.
>
> On the other hand, this over-functionalization carries with it certain liabilities which have not been generally recognized. For one thing, it brings together in one place large numbers of employees on the same job level. Where the job level is low, as it is in many cases, this concentration makes the organization much more vulnerable to personnel difficulties than would be the case if such jobs were scattered among several departments representing a greater variety of activities and job levels.[18]

[15] See author's Ph.D. dissertation, *Grievances and Union Management Relations*, Department of Economics and Social Science, Massachusetts Institute of Technology, 1950.

[16] In a very interesting study, Dreyfus observes that it is possible to prevent the development of any feeling of solidarity among white collar workers by artificially complicating the job titles and rankings within a group (complications that have no real meaning in terms of skill or earnings differences). Carl Dreyfus, "Prestige Grading: A Mechanism of Control," in *Reader in Bureaucracy*, edited by R. K. Merton, Free Press, Glencoe, Ill., 1952, pp. 258–264.

[17] A. K. Rice, "Productivity and Social Organization in an Indian Weaving Shed," *Human Relations*, VI, 1953, p. 310.

[18] James Worthy, "Factors Influencing Employee Morale," *Harvard Business Review*, XXVIII, 1950, p. 70.

The significance of these differentiating factors (job, service, age, sex, nationality) lies in the fact that the more bases there are for differentiation within a collectivity, the less likelihood there is for any one group to separate out.[19]

From three quite different points of view, researchers and administrators have observed that concentrations of employees, with only a minimum of differentiating factors, are more likely to result in united, self-interest behavior.

The psychologist would explain such behavior in the following terms.[20] Within the setting of a group of colleagues who share similar points of view there is a mutual reinforcement of the sentiments each holds individually. Feelings are intensified by the group process. In fact, as shared attitudes are reinforced in this manner, there is a tendency for some distortion in member perception to take place. Inequities appear greater, management motives perhaps more evil, the union leader even less responsive. The familiar process by which a mass movement oversimplifies and highlights common problems is part of this resonance effect. And finally the recognition that one's own feelings are simultaneously shared by fellow employees lifts inhibitions which otherwise would restrain concerted action. Many years of instilled respect for the boss, his orders, and for property deter the individual from aggressive activity; but with the sanction of his group, in fact, with its positive approval, his possible guilt feelings are overcome and he acts strongly, often with the moral and physical support of his fellows.

Although we have no evidence on the point, we can speculate about the effect of divided group loyalties on group pressure tactics. Following some observations in the printing trades, it appears likely that men who must work closely together have some tendency to deemphasize or repress discussions and activities concerning areas where there may be disagreement among themselves.[21]

[19] F. J. Roethlisberger and W. Dickson, *Management and the Worker*, Harvard University Press, Cambridge, 1939, p. 539.

[20] This part of the analysis is suggested by Professor Ross Stagnar's comments on the group process in *Psychology of Conflict*, John Wiley and Sons, New York, 1956, p. 9.

[21] A recent study in printing shops indicates that where there is any degree of political disagreement, union political discussions are deemphasized. The researchers note that this trend is particularly true in small shops where the men must *involuntarily* associate with a given group. In larger shops one is better able to select his work group friends on the basis of similarity of political interest, so that there is not the need to repress political discussion for the sake of group harmony. These authors observe that involuntary interaction (in the small shop) is more constrained. There is the need to limit discussion to those

Thus in groups which lack occupational homogeneity, but which must continue to function as a highly interdependent team (with contacts predetermined by the work process), the members may discover that attempts to gain a consensus on "what should we do about our problems" will lead to animosity and friction. The only means of avoiding or at least minimizing the resulting tensions is to avoid these topics themselves. As a result, they may take substantially less concerted action than we would predict on the basis of their individual levels of discontent. It is only in those areas where all can agree (e.g., less work for everybody) that group activity is possible. Yet the realities of the grievance process are such that only highly specific grievances (e.g., the classification rate or production rate on a particular job) have much chance of gaining successful prosecution. Where everyone has exactly the same job, there is no need to repress discussions of job problems for the sake of group harmony. They can continue to live together and still agree on common modes of action.

THE ESSENTIALNESS OF THEIR FUNCTION

There is a broad distinction between plants where the work in all departments is highly interrelated and where work groups can function rather autonomously. The two extremes are the job shop in which each department has a distinct job which does not relate to nor tie in with the work of any other department, and the continuous assembly line where no work can be done unless everyone is producing at an appropriate rate. Most organizations fall somewhere in the middle of these extremes, and various work groups within these companies have differing degrees of indispensability to the product of the total labor force.

Certain groups who perform operations in the production sequence can more easily halt total plant operations than can other groups. This ability is predicated on certain features of the work flow. For example, there are areas within an automobile plant where completed work, which cannot proceed as scheduled to the next work station, can be stored. In other areas, due to the construction of the lines and the bulk of the unit in manufacture, storage is out of the question. Therefore, when the group just "ahead" in the processing flow lays

---

subjects upon which all can agree for the sake of peaceful relations. On the other hand, in a group where one has more freedom to select his on-the-job friends (because the work process does not predetermine with whom one has to interact) workers will be more likely to form themselves into politically lively interest groups. Seymour Lipset, Martin Trow, and James Coleman, *Union Democracy*, Free Press, Glencoe, Ill., 1956, pp. 166, 171–175.

down its tools, all the preceding operations must stop. There is no place for the completed work to go. There are similar production stages in non-assembly-line manufacturing processes. Lacking any adequate "bank" of materials with which to work, other areas close down almost simultaneously with these bottleneck operations.

The data show that true job shops are less likely to exhibit concerted action such as is typical of Strategic and Erratic groups. The latter are found primarily in plants where there is some flow of work between departments.

In a more specific example, those feeder lines which were somewhat independent of the main line (that is, they could build up a bank of finished parts and did not have to stop if the main line shut down) seemed *less* prone to engage in stoppages themselves than did the groups which were more tightly tied to the line. It is conceivable that these relatively independent groups built up less tension as a result of the activities of the main line (where stoppages did occur), and therefore less resentment about losing time and earnings, than those groups whose fate was completely in the hands of the main line.

There was also a tendency for groups at the very beginning (e.g., shearsmen) and the very end (e.g., packaging personnel) of production lines to be more inclined to press grievances and engage in concerted behavior than similar work groups (in terms of number and types of jobs) nearer the middle of the production process. In a sense, the beginning and end groups are in a slightly more essential position.

Another example of an essential group involves the critical *materials handlers* who handle goods in transit. Truckers and cranemen usually have the distinction of sharing this enviable position, and management, at least, believes this explains their strong bargaining propensities.

It is somewhat more difficult to assess the "criticalness" of certain skilled occupational groups. On occasion, management makes a statement such as this: "We don't worry when they go out in Department Y; we can bring in other men from other work areas who have had experience there, or train new people in a short period of time. Let them walk off the job over in Department X, however, and they've got us—those men can't be replaced."

While the complexity and skill required by the job is one factor in ease of replacement, there is also the important matter of fellow-worker and union support of the grievance. In many instances the problems of an individual group do *not* muster the support of other workers. The balance of the work force reports for duty and carries on normal activities. Nevertheless, if the strikers are actually replaced by transfers from other departments, the issue may spread.

However, except for immediately adjacent groups, our research showed little evidence that one work group actively courted the support of another. Although workers often referred to the excellence of support or the treasonable lack of it, the relationships among concerted interest areas were not sufficiently well developed to foster any extensive exchange of favors. (On the other side of the picture, work groups that were isolated from other employees, both geographically and in terms of the flow of work, rarely played a key role in plant affairs.)

Most interesting was the lack of any apparent friction over loss of earnings opportunities due to the actions of some other group. For example, in automobile manufacturing it is taken as a matter of course that two or three dozen key truckers or trimmers who are struggling with some personal issue will idle thousands of fellow employees. It should be noted, however, that the loss of work on the part of nonstriking employees is usually due to the production bottleneck created by the strikers, and not to sympathetic action.

In any case, there is wide variation in the possibilities. Thus "criticalness of skill" depends on intrinsic job characteristics as well as fellow-worker support in adjacent work areas. The latter depends on the respect which the particular group has won (based in part on its support of other groups) and the general unity prevailing in the shop community, which rests upon mutual support given and received.

Since management makes no secret of the fact that certain operations are more indispensable, or less expendable, than those in nearby work areas of a less critical nature, it is to be expected that some of the most essential groups will take advantage of their leverage.[22]

Most observers have felt that there is some relationship between essentialness of location and the self-confidence demonstrated by a given work group. As in the case of a previously discussed variable, the position on the promotional ladder, management's willingness to concede on many issues often disguises the data. That is, a group which might conceivably demonstrate continuous pressure need not

[22] Cf. "The productive arrangements of a given plant place certain operations in a technically strategic position. . . . The strategic position of such workers, reflected frequently in their importance in internal union politics, is likely to constitute a factor contributing to a more favorable treatment obtained from management and more active negotiations conducted on their behalf by union leaders." Martin Segal, "Factors in Wage Adjustment to Technological Changes," *Industrial and Labor Relations Review*, VIII, 1955, p. 225.

do so, because its indispensability causes desired adjustments to come relatively easily. This factor undoubtedly contributes to the bargaining power of the group. The data indicate that the "chances for success," to whatever attributable, bulk large in a work group's decision to engage in or refrain from concerted activity.[23] However, in this respect, they are somewhat secondary to other determinants, those that shape the "sense of inequity," the feeling that something *ought* to be done, or, as is often true in the case of Erratic groups, the inability to control behavior that might lead to other alternative approaches to the problems at hand.

WORK STANDARDS INVOLVING JUDGMENT

Another common characteristic of a substantial number of the groups noted for high activity (Strategic and Erratic) is the fact that their work standards involve elements of judgment. By judgment, we mean simply that there are aspects of the job that are not subject to complete specifications and analysis; the worker cannot be told in advance exactly what to do and, more importantly, cannot be told exactly how long the work should take. In other words, production standards are difficult, and almost impossible in some cases, to set with complete precision. As a result of this judgment factor, the worker and in turn the work group gain certain controls over the job that make concerted action potentially worthwile; obviously the area of bargainable standards is relatively broad in these cases.

This factor also contributes to the worker's evaluation of his skill level. In nearly all the middle groups, characterized by high activity and consciousness of unrecognized status, the judgment required in their work was one of the most significant elements which justified their claim to be included among the highly skilled.

This same factor also enhanced the workers' freedom from supervisors and time-study men, which contributed to their self-image as skilled craftsmen. Stories are legion, such as these:

> Holter, the day shift foreman, came up and told me to speed up the machines. I looked at him as if he were crazy, but still followed the order. I couldn't wait for what I knew was going to happen—the whole thing to jam up and the work to be ruined. That's the thing about these machines; it takes years to know what they'll do, each one is different and has to be babied, and none of the damn' supervisors can tell you how to run them—they just don't know themselves; it doesn't follow the book.

[23] This factor will be further explored in the following chapter.

A superintendent made this comment:

> We know our time studies for welders don't mean much. They can always fiddle around with the air pressure or the quantity of acetylene. We tried locking the valves, but they always find a way of speeding up or slowing down the operation by adjusting their tools.

As we have already indicated, management often admitted its inability to set accurate standards on these jobs. The usual result is either exceptionally high earnings or unwarranted leisure. Which of these gains the workers choose depends to a considerable extent on other factors in the situation.

Chinoy, in his study of an automobile plant, found that employees are very conscious of the advantageousness of jobs that lack clearly defined efficiency standards:

> For many off-production tasks, no fixed quantitative standards of performance exist against which foremen can measure the efforts of their workers, though they must obviously maintain some standards of efficiency. "That's the advantage of a job off production," said a truckdriver. "There is no set amount of work you have to do. You aren't pushed or crowded like on production." [24]

Serious problems are likely to occur in that middle ground between jobs which are obviously machine- or management-paced and jobs over which the employee retains a large degree of controls, as is true of craft occupations. A good example in the middle range is the trim line in plants manufacturing automobile bodies. Management has developed extensive time studies to support the speed at which the line moves—all without worker control. But employees in the department have never given up insisting that the time studies are not accurate, that the recalcitrance of trim materials (cloth), and the "judgmental qualities of their job" make many of these studies inaccurate.[25] The continuous struggle caused by the differences between the rates set by management and the rates demanded by employees is one of the outstanding sources of wildcat strikes in the automobile industry.[26]

We found that workers with jobs whose production standards could be set unequivocally were unlikely to engage in concerted in-

[24] Chinoy, *op. cit.*, p. 72.

[25] Cf. previous chapter, p. 30.

[26] The usual pattern is for several employees to work at a slower pace than defined by management. After they have been warned that they will have to work faster and "keep up with the line," and they fail to change their pace, penalties are assessed. The ensuing strike, then, is a formal protest over the disciplinary penalties, and not over the work rates.

terest behavior to the extent demonstrated by workers whose standards depended on this judgment factor. At the other end of the spectrum maintenance and craft workers, with perhaps the greatest degree of freedom to set their own pace, did not concentrate so much effort on improving their jobs as those in the middle groups. Again it was the middle groups, those whose jobs were in many ways relatively routine production operations, who devoted themselves to self-interest activity. These were the jobs on which management and employees were most likely to differ on the matter of a "fair day's work." Welding, metal finishing, trim work, and similar operations, where worker judgment was involved, played a disproportionately heavy share in plant grievance activity and in other pressure devices designed to obtain concessions on work load matters.

Another type of job, between craft work and completely machined-paced operations, is that which involves technological imperfections. In operations like electrolytic refining of metal or metal plating, there are frequently several uncontrolled technical factors which affect the quantity of output in relation to employee effort. Particularly where an incentive plan is involved, a spate of process difficulties can set off a chain reaction. Earnings are less than expected and employees become resentful, frequently focusing their discontent on the work standards, which are declared "unfair." This resentment probably further diminishes output and management, in reacting to this, places direct pressure on supervision and employees to bring up their output levels. The increase in downward-directed pressure can result in a further decrement in output on the part of employees, causing, in turn, more management pressure. Thus, a sharp, downward spiraling productivity curve can begin with a modest technical problem, and work standard grievances are an additional by-product. On this type of operations there is usually ample justification, in the eyes of employees, that standards are unfair, since output and bonus earnings are unpredictable. This attitude provides fertile ground for pressure group activity. Because of the crew nature of many of these operations and the high degree of worker interdependence, combined with an uncertain flow of work, Erratic pressure group behavior is a frequent concomitant.

REPETITIVENESS OF THE TASK

We found no clear-cut relationship between job repetitiveness and work group grievances. It might have been expected that routine, repetitive operations involving greater monotony and absorbing less worker attentiveness than non-routine operations, would be more likely to breed aggressive activity. If anything, there is some evidence that the opposite expectation is more tenable. Non-routine work areas demonstrated a higher frequency of concerted behavior in those plants where such differences could be compared. There were two plants which had almost identical work departments, some of which were engaged in routine and others in non-routine production (their product mix was more varied). (The level of skills required, were, of course, very similar.) In both cases, the "routine" areas were the more peaceful.

Speculatively, we might suggest that the non-routine area was more likely to create production-originated tensions involving both technical and scheduling matters. These would be fruitful sources of grievances and disagreement. Standards would probably be ambiguous, and, in addition, non-routine operations are likely to encourage close supervision, a source of resentment.

Also, non-routine jobs may require "surface attention"—the need for the worker to concentrate enough to make daydreaming impossible, but offering him insufficient inherent challenge to provide real absorption in the job and intrinsic job satisfaction.

This generalization does not hold for interplant comparisons, that is, where one plant operates on a job-shop basis and another on straight production runs. Here other factors come into the picture because most job shops have work groups which are structured differently from those in continuous production, as noted in the previous section.

COMPACTNESS

Management and the union often assume that putting workers closer together accentuates problems. Undoubtedly, there is a point beyond which increased crowding leads to both internal group frictions and more grievances expressed outwardly to management. This is the point at which people have difficulty in moving around on the job without limiting the freedom of movement of a fellow employee. Certainly at some stations on automobile assembly lines, where output had been stepped up substantially by the addition of new personnel, these crowded conditions prevailed. Union officials spoke frankly about certain areas as being "hot spots" because of this space situation.

Over a wide range of variation, however, there was no correlation between the compactness of the group and its behavior pattern. It will be recalled that "scatter groups," distributed throughout an entire plant or number of plants, on occasion could be as vocal and active as the members of other departments which were located in compact geographic areas.

SEX DIFFERENCES

A previous study by the author noted that women are in some respects "disenfranchised" in many industrial unions, not by specific policy or intent but by the force of cultural values.[27] Furthermore, women are somewhat more reluctant than men to participate in a union and may be more reluctant to engage in persistent aggressive actions. In the course of this study there certainly seemed to be some tendency for work groups with a high proportion of female employees to be more passive and restrained than their male counterparts. Nevertheless, those female groups that we expected, on the basis of the other criteria, to produce high activity, often fulfilled the prediction. Where they did not, it could also be due to a greater preponderance of short service, temporary employees within the female group.

However, we had the opportunity to observe only a few male and female groups that were technologically similar and these are tentative conclusions.

HOURS OF WORK

The hours of work are another factor which seem to have only a minor impact on the behavior of work groups. Employees on other but the day shift have in common the problem of adjusting their daily routine to unusual working hours. As Lipset points out, they may be drawn together in the need for shared social activities within periods of the day when most people are still at work.[28] In many plants supervision is less stringent in the evenings; major problems of change are tackled during the day, and the organization of the night shift is substantially more informal than in daytime.

All of these factors tend to make the night shift into more of an entity than the day shift. Consequently sharp differentiations among work groups are *less* in evidence, as are their special interest pressures.

SUMMARY

We have tried to explain the kinds of differences we observed in work group behavior. Our explanation has not resulted in any simple

[27] Sayles and Strauss, *op. cit.*, pp. 211–215.
[28] Lipset, *op. cit.*, p. 102.

formula for predicting work group response to management and the union. We found a number of characteristics that seem to bear a relationship to the categories we discussed in the previous chapter. The *degree of activity*, whether tending toward the passive or toward the continuously active, seems to be influenced by relatively objective variables, such as the following:

1. Relative position on the promotional "ladders" of the plant.
2. Relative size and importance of the group.
3. Similarity of jobs within the group.
4. The degree to which their work is indispensable in the functioning of the plant or department.
5. The precision with which management can measure work load and pace for the group.

The repetitiveness of the task, the hours of work, the density of the work force (ratio of men to machines within a given area), and the sex distribution within the group seemed to be of substantially less importance in explaining behavior differences.

We would conclude that the highest incidence of grievance activity occurs in middle rung job groups. These are jobs, in pay and prestige, substantially above the starting jobs in the plant, and on which workers feel they have some chance of prospering. (The operations in this range are usually included in the Erratic and Strategic job groups.)

These groups have certain elements in common. The jobs, all considered relatively desirable by employees in the plants visited, are popular, but they are not the best in the plant. They are the middle-class occupations of the industrial plants we surveyed.

The middle rung is composed of relatively prominent occupational groups within the plant, employing a significant number of workers. That is, they are not isolated occupations with only a few employees. However, there were several notable exceptions. These we termed "island groups," which were small pockets or concentrations of one occupational group, surrounded by other, foreign occupational groups.

In a substantial number of instances, perhaps half of the cases investigated, we observed that where there are strong, active work groups, there is a significant element of worker control in the production process, that is, the operations are not completely "machine paced" and time studies are less likely to be tight. There is more room for maneuvering, insofar as management cannot completely control all the job conditions, for example, the number of passes the operator must make, how high he has his torch turned up or even the speed with which he operates his machines. Put in another way, the possible fruits of individual or group action are greater because of the inherent flexibility in the work itself.

Management spokesmen as well as union spokesmen often referred to a group's position in the flow of work as contributing to its bellicosity or aggressiveness. The reasoning goes, if a group feels it can shut down the plant, it is more likely to "put the pressure on." Undoubtedly, such logic does have some impact on the group's thinking, particularly if in the past management has readily conceded an issue where the group's criticalness seemed to be a prime consideration. This would explain the relative frequency of truckers' wildcats in the automobile industry, where many companies depend on tightly coordinated hourly deliveries to maintain production. However, in most plants the number of groups that can shut down production is relatively large. This is the case in assembly operations where each station is as critical as the next (with the possible exception of some jobs which are more difficult to fill than others). Therefore, the question why one group is active rather than another remains significant. Strategic position may be one of the necessary, but not sufficient, conditions for successful grievance activity.

B. Internal Organization of the Work Group

Technology also shapes the relationships within the work group, and thus the structure of the group itself. It is at this more microcosmic level that we shall find other factors of interest in explaining differences in the behavior of groups within the industrial plant. What are the differences between groups comprised of individual jobs, on which employees do not have to cooperate with one another in the work process, and assembly lines and crews, which are interdependent operations?

In our case descriptions in the preceding chapter of typical work groups that comprised our four basic behavior "types," we noted certain concentrations related to their internal organizational structure (the interaction pattern imposed by the technology of the plant). The accompanying table summarizes these findings.

To a large extent these differences in the organization of the work team or work unit are determined by the manner in which the technological system ties workers together. There is some indication at

Behavior Pattern	Interaction Pattern of the Job	Behavior Exhibited
Apathetic	Individual jobs—primarily mixed departments where there are no concentrations of employees doing identical tasks Mixed crews (members have different tasks) Long assembly lines	Essentially passive, high activity only on special occasions
Erratic	Crew operations, with all members performing similar tasks Short assembly lines	Unstable, highly demonstrative, volatile
Strategic	Individual operations Some homogenous crew or assembly operations	Persistent self-interest activity which is of a calculated type
Conservative	Individual operations, including many scatter jobs	Self-interest causes restrained

least that *interdependence* among workers, imposed by the flow-of-work, reduces the likelihood that a particular group will show high concerted activity in the grievance process.

A notable exception was the type of groups we have referred to as homogeneous crews. Here a number of men, utilizing exactly the same skills, worked with one another in performing a given task. The trimmers and the strippers are good cases in point. In fact, a number of operating units we classified as Erratic were homogeneous crews.

Another exception, although a less common one, involved homogeneous assembly operation: tub polishers, torch solderers, and metal finishers. In these groups, men worked on an assembly line performing operations that were almost identical, but each man contributed an additional element to the finished product.

The behavior of the homogeneous crews and assembly lines contrasted sharply with that of crews and assembly lines in which the members performed quite different tasks.

In this section therefore we want to explore somewhat more systematically how the behavior of integrated work teams differs from the behavior of groups of employees whose individual members perform their duties independently.

DIFFERENTIATION OF TASK

One of the most obvious distinctions between "individual" jobs and crew or assembly jobs is the factor of job differentiation. Most of the individual jobs we observed involved a number of employees doing similar tasks. In fact, if their work was not similar we found notable passivity (Apathetic groups). Almost by definition, however, most crews and assembly lines (there are those exceptions discussed previously) involve the working together of a group of individuals, each of whom is doing a slightly different task. What impact does this type of work flow system have on what we have called internal homogeneity or resonance?

1. *Diminishes Grievance Reinforcement.* It may reduce unity within the group, as Chandler points out in her excellent case study of a work group that experienced a methods change which converted individual independent jobs into an assembly operation.

> Moreover, the changeover from the section to the line system destroyed the old bargaining groupings of the workers. Formerly, workers performing the same operation sat together in groups and were able to compare their daily earnings easily. The frontmakers were among the strongest of all the groups in pressing their grievances in the days of the section work system, but under the line system, there was no such thing as a frontmaker. The operations were divided into much smaller parts, and a worker was placed in a line where there were at most only one or two other persons performing her operation. The union manager opposed these changes partly because she felt that the line system would weaken the operators' day-to-day bargaining position. She described the effect of the change:
>
> "The line system places the workers in a competitive situation. It destroys cooperation between them, and puts one worker against another, and one line against the other. Each line is a unit. No line cares what happens to the others."
>
> Most workers felt that the introduction of the line system increased the problems connected with grievance formulation. One of them remarked:
>
> "I know they never have two lines on the same style in the same plant because that keeps the girls from getting together on things. Nobody cares about anybody's style or problems but their own. A grievance is usually confined to one line and to one, two, or three workers on that line who are doing a particular operation. If there are two girls on an operation, it is easier because then you have someone to back you up. If a girl is all alone, she has a tough time." [29]

Thus, a division of labor which separates or eliminates workers doing identical tasks, reduces their tendency to engage in concerted activity. The number of problems on which there can be consensus has been reduced by the simple expedient of reducing the number of similar jobs, or so separating them in space that communications barriers are erected among the jobholders.

[29] Chandler, *op. cit.,* pp. 479–481.

On the other hand, in the case of *homogeneous crews*, the resonance factor may be magnified. Every experience is shared almost simultaneously because the work causes such a high level of worker interaction. Such complete and immediate sharing could explain partially the tendency for such groups to be spontaneously rather than strategically active.

The combination of several interrelated jobs (and status levels) in the typical work crew may serve to diminish concerted action for still another reason. Many of the jobs discussed earlier that were concentration points for grievances were also the realistic top of the promotional ladder for the job incumbents. Above these jobs only a few highly selective opportunities for promotion occurred. However, the work crew traditionally has incorporated its own internal promotional ladder. The jobs are arranged in order of progression up to crew chief, and promotions are not only likely but expected of all crew members.

2. *Complicates Social Structure.* The second consequence of job differentiation (the first was the tendency to reduce the resonance factor) is to complicate the social structure of the group. This results from two sources.

On the basis of the Western Electric studies, as well as succeeding work, we know that different jobs carry with them different prestige or status values. Whatever the common currency in the plant for valuing work, the distinctions within a work crew or assembly group are usually sufficient to cause some of the jobs to be rated higher than others. This ranking may or may not be reflected in pay differentials. The incumbents on the job, in turn, take on some of the status characteristics associated with their jobs.

For example, in the well known Bank Wiring Room study, the manufacture of "banks of terminals" for central office telephone equipment involved at one stage the close cooperation of wiremen, soldermen, and inspectors. Beginners were usually placed on soldering, then promoted to the wiring job.[30] In this department a good deal of illegal job trading took place and it was observed: "In practically every case, the request for a trade came from the wireman, and the solderman concerned traded without protest."[31] In other words, the individual in the higher status job, felt that it was more appropriate for him to propose this trade than did an employee in the lower status job. This situation was independent of the personality charac-

[30] George Homans, *The Human Group*, Harcourt Brace, New York, 1950, p. 58.
[31] *Ibid.*, p. 67.

teristics of the individuals concerned. Similarly, at another point in the study the original authors noted:

> Examining the internal organization of the group from this point of view it will be seen that there was some correspondence between occupation and position in the group. This undoubtedly accounted for the position held by the trucker. He was relegated to the most subordinate position in the room, *not because of any personal characteristic but simply because he was a trucker.*[32] [Italics mine.]

And, as they observed later, "It may be concluded that occupational status was one of the important factors entering into the determination of the individual's position in the group." [33]

Workers in an interdependent work group are presumably not able to interact freely with whomever they wish. Put in another way, intrinsic personality characteristics are less the determining factor of whom the worker talks to, when, where, and how often, than the work process which requires that he spend more time with some people than with others, and may actually specify his entire interaction pattern.

It would appear that limitations are placed on the individual's adjustment to the work situation by the status position and interaction position predetermined by the technology of the job. While we know of no studies which have explored the matter directly, we can hypothesize that groups in which the members are "confined" are more subject to internal frictions (and subsequent weakness in their strength vis-à-vis management and the union) than groups in which members are free to adjust their social relations with one another on the basis of temperament and need. We do know that interdependent work operations are subject to internal strife; we are not sure of the source of this friction, however.

Worker X, because of the relation of his job to that of Worker Y must constantly respond to Y and also must assume a somewhat subordinate position to Y. Depending on X's personality, this adjustment may or may not be a relatively easy thing for him to do. The situation suggests that there may be a likelihood of personal friction, if an individual employee is not free to adopt a role (relating himself to the work group) that will be a good "fit" for his personality.

Nevertheless, the evidence is conflicting. The existence of relatively unambiguous "roles" relating individuals in the work group to one another may actually be a positive factor in intragroup relations. The definiteness of the structure may eliminate some of the uncer-

[32] Roethlisberger and Dickson, *op. cit.*, p. 514.
[33] *Ibid.*, p. 516.

tainties, the pullings and haulings that result from ambiguity in role designation. For example, in groups unstructured by the technology there may be real in-group problems, created by "usurpers," who are seeking informal leadership.[34] In more structured groups the internal status system is also fixed by job title and activity.

Secondly, at least two studies purport to show that workers are less restricted than we have assumed by flow-of-work relations. On the basis of these studies there seems to be substantial leeway on interdependent jobs for employees to relate themselves to others and to adopt a personally satisfying social role in the group.

Arensberg and Horsfall, on the basis of their very careful observations of interaction among four similar work teams, conclude that there was little in common among the internal interaction pattern other than that all of the teams could be defined as "groups of people who interacted more frequently with one another than with others as a result of the controlling effects of the flow of work." [35]

> However, in internal structures the teams were not collections of people bound together by quantitatively uniform relationships, insofar as their measured interaction pattern was concerned. The facts were quite to the contrary. Internally, the teams were collections of relatively inactive persons ranged about clusters of highly interactive persons, only one or two in each team, serving as a center or nexus for the rest. Members differed widely in their rates of activity with one another; some of them responsive mostly to immediate neighbors, some of them serving as targets or confidants for a wider circle taking in most of the group, some of them very alert to persons outside. The groups were "structured," then, around only the more active or more widely responsive of their members. *Factors influencing such structuring will by no means be uniform, as far as could be judged, without special study.* Central special position among the workers of a team vied with leadership function in the over-all organization of the room allocation system. This was the main reason why in the teams one person or another served as such focal point. *Personality factors seem to determine whether one was to act as such a nexus in a favorable spacial position, just as personality factors coupled with status differences seem to indicate why it was that the two informal leaders of the room were among the oldest and most experienced of the men workers, in a room full of less skilled boys and women.*[36] [Italics mine.]

In a similar manner Miller attempted in a unique study to investigate the relation between the job definition of glass blowing (according to technological specifications) and the interaction pattern of the indi-

[34] Cf. the attempts of one of the wiremen (w6) in the bank wiring study to achieve group leadership. *Ibid.*, p. 519.

[35] A. B. Horsfall and C. M. Arensberg, "Teamwork and Productivity in a Shoe Factory," *Human Organization*, VIII, 1949, p. 22.

[36] *Ibid.*, p. 22.

viduals holding those jobs. Miller concludes, "We found no statistically significant *correspondence* in patterns of any of the top three positions (of the crews studied)."[37]

Even more interesting, Miller showed that the greatest variety in the on-the-job behavior for any occupational group was for the crew chiefs in the department surveyed, who had more elements of their job in common with one another than did the incumbents on any other job!

Thus, we are not sure how this combination of unique jobs and unique personalities is likely to affect interpersonal relations within the work group.

FREQUENCY OF INTERACTION

We have considered differences in the rigidity of interworker relationships contributed by differences in interaction patterns between independent and non-interdependent work areas. There is another element in the interaction pattern, however.

By definition, jobs in crews and assembly lines require constant interaction. The technology inherent in these jobs demands a much more intimate, intense "living together" than is required for employees who work independently. We would suggest that work experience has greater saliency or emotional content in the interdependent work situation. What meaning would this have for concerted action?

1. *Difficulty in Combining into Large Action Units.* A recent study of small mining crews by a group of British social scientists states the case well:

> It would appear that the self-enclosed character of the relationship makes it difficult for groups of this kind to combine effectively in differentiated structures of a somewhat larger social magnitude. . . .[38]

The authors note that this small crew structure did not prevent their combination at the community level, but only at what they call the intermediate level (which would correspond to the factory).

Each crew or short assembly line (where it is short enough to combine at all) can become really a world to itself.[39] The close ties of the members to this work unit make loyalty to some larger interest group difficult to sustain.

[37] Frank B. Miller, *Expanding the Scope of Case Study Research by Interaction Counting* (mimeographed), Cornell University, Ithaca, N. Y., 1953, p. 44*A*.

[38] E. L. Trist and E. W. Bamforth, "Social and Psychological Consequences of the Longwall Method of Coal-getting," *Human Relations*, IV, 1951, p. 8.

[39] Cf. Chandler *op. cit.*, p. 532.

The work crew is so much an entity in itself that it has difficulty in combining with similar work crews with which it may have a natural mutuality of interest. We saw repeatedly the inability of identical teams to work together for common goals. Even when they did reach informal agreement, their conformity failed to live up to expectations. The failure to attain the objective agreed upon then dampened further efforts and we would hear: "Well, what can you expect; they don't care anything about us!" Following is a typical case involving a substitute worker:

> He normally worked with an adjacent team, but an absence caused his temporary transfer. After the first day he voiced his surprise at the fact that the crew to which he was temporarily assigned lacked some of the excellent equipment possessed by his own team in the same department. When he attempted to urge this team to demand equitable treatment from management he was summarily hushed by the statement: "What difference does it make to you anyhow, you don't work here normally!"

Longer assembly lines, on which workers are restricted in their interaction to workers on either side of them, may also inhibit the development of any real informal group, as Walker and Guest observed in their study of automobile assembly lines.[40] Another recent study finds that assembly lines encourage the formation of tightly knit *pairs* of workers which, in turn, results in a number of operators being socially isolated. Zaleznik, in a study of an assembly line consisting of 35 workers "stationed at a moving belt doing simple wiring and soldering operations" found:

> An operator could talk easily only with workers on her immediate right and left. From the point of view of any one worker, her only possible spontaneous group during working hours consisted of two workers and herself, or a group of three. A threesome, however, tends to make a very unstable group because of the likelihood of pairing. It is easy therefore, for some operators at least to find themselves socially isolated . . . Once something goes wrong, there is considerable interaction, but under conditions of extreme tension and anxiety.[41]

On the basis of such findings we would conclude that assembly lines are *not* conducive to the formation of cohesive, inclusive worker groups.

2. *Multiple Affiliations—Conflict between the Team Unit and the Occupational Unit.* In those cases where the work team was made up

[40] Charles R. Walker and Robert Guest, *The Man on the Assembly Line,* Harvard University Press, Cambridge, 1952, p. 79.

[41] A. Zaleznik, *Worker Satisfaction and Development,* Harvard University Graduate School of Business Administration, Boston, 1956, pp. 120–121.

of different skills, the men vacillated between identifying themselves with occupational groups (e.g., the hammersmiths) and with their work teams (e.g., the hammershop work team). There was frequently a conflict between concentrating efforts on improving team benefits and those of the specific job classification of which one was a member.

In steel crews this simple question was often an enigma:

> Should I work to increase my incentive earnings by increasing the percentage of the group's earnings to which I am entitled, or should I work to increase the total "pie" by seeking better or looser incentive rates, my proportion of which would remain constant?

This conflict was very evident in interviews with the men. "With what group should I identify?" In practice, of course, there was identification both ways, but this divided loyalty may very well have been the cause of a basic weakness in the heterogeneous groups. Such a situation certainly was not true among some of the homogeneous crews and these departments were, in fact, substantially more active and successful in prosecuting their demands (some as Erratic and some as Strategic groups).

3. *Inadequate Frequency of Interaction.* We have been exploring some of the ramifications of a high frequency of interaction among work group members. In the previous chapter we referred to some Erratic behavior groups whose outstanding characteristic was their inability to communicate sufficiently to enable them to perform their task effectively. These were areas in the plant we termed points of blind coordination, where two or more groups of workers needed to coordinate their efforts on an almost minute-to-minute basis, but were so located that this was impossible. Lacking an adequate frequency of interaction, we judged that work-derived tensions accumulated until some explosion occurred, which was as likely to be directed against management as against fellow workers.

These are cases in which the social unit (or the informal group) is smaller or less inclusive than the work unit. What is essentially a single stage in the production process is artificially divided by the plant layout.[42]

Researchers at Tavistock have been interested in a similar problem.[43]

[42] Dr. Eliot Chapple has called attention to the frictions that normally occur at any point in the production process where there is a *change* in the pacing of the flow of work: for example, where materials from one process are collected and shipped over to another process.

[43] Trist and Bamforth, *op. cit.*, pp. 3–37. A. K. Rice, "Productivity and Social Organization in an Indian Weaving Shed," *Human Relations*, VI, 1953, pp. 297–329.

They find that frictions and discontent at the work place are reduced when the work team incorporates all individuals whose work is highly interdependent. They studied cases, in coal mining and textile weaving in which workers, whose activities were directly interrelated, were separated from one another by management's formal organization of production. Under these circumstances, the intimate communications and self-control mechanisms of the work group do not function efficiently: one individual tends to blame another (whom he does not know) for failure to complete the work quota and for other shortcomings of coordination. Recriminations build onto one another and grievances follow. However, when those who are interdependent work closely together, the informal group itself produces the needed adjustments and interpersonal coordinations required by the work process.

Thus, the frequency of interaction can militate against sustained, well contrived economic interest behavior at both the high and the low end of the scale. Where interworker contacts are very high within a group which is smaller than the natural unit of self-improvement (e.g., where there are a number of similar crews in a department), narrow, parochial interests may throttle the possibility of uniting for larger issues. These groups are likely to demonstrate Apathetic behavior. On the other hand, where the work unit is artificially divided by some physical communications barrier, work-derived discontents are constantly boiling over and giving these areas a reputation for Erratic behavior. Of course, both behavior types may guarantee ineffectual grievance handling.

THE PROBLEM OF GAINING AGREEMENT ON OUTPUT STANDARDS IN THE INTERDEPENDENT GROUP

There are at least two other aspects of member behavior in teams which may affect the group's cohesiveness. As we have noted earlier, and as has been amply documented in a number of studies, work group members are expected to adhere to certain standards of output or production which the group as a whole has approved.[44] We know that within a group of workers physical abilities differ, that financial needs differ (and concomitantly the need for incentive earnings, merit increases, and promotion), and also that personal standards of what is desirable conduct in the industrial situation differ.[45] On individual operations these differences can have somewhat freer sway. To be

[44] Cf. Roethlisberger and Dickson, *op. cit.*, p. 517. Seashore, *op. cit.*, pp. 15–22.

[45] William F. Whyte and others, *Money and Motivation*, Harpers, New York, 1955, pp. 39–48.

sure, there will be informal pressures on recalcitrant "rate busters," but the determined independents can go it alone to a reasonable extent. However, by the very nature of a crew or assembly operation, the output of the individual must be correlated with the output of the group.

It is equally apparent that the decisions as to how much effort should be expended, what level of earnings is appropriate (assuming some system of payment by results), and how closely the group should adhere to management standards, are highly important ones for a production crew, just because deviation from the approved level is almost impossible.

The same conditions hold for employees of the assembly operation, although their task is complicated enormously by the structure of the assembly line. Except on the very short lines, the social group on the assembly line bears no correspondence to the production unit. It thus becomes difficult for the members of an assembly line to control output. Unfortunately, however, we know little of how crews or assembly lines reach a decision on appropriate output standards.[46]

While a crew is compelled to achieve some substantial degree of agreement on job standards, the process may not be a simple one because of the very nature of the crew structure. There are several types of problems involved, which are illustrated by the discussion which follows.

(1) In a steel plant, a forging or hammer crew is paid primarily on the basis of tonnage produced. Shares in the bonus earned are distributed on the basis of the level of skill contributed by each member of the crew as measured by the job evaluation system. Thus the crew chief and his helper receive nearly double the bonus share of the other crew members. Many of the lesser skilled members are reluctant to agree to increased production because they feel "most of our increased earnings go to those fellows so why should we work that much harder?"

(2) For many crews, increased work does not affect each member of the team identically. For some, the additional work adds to their job burden much more than the same quantity of increased production adds to the job burden of other members of the same team.

[46] At this point it should not be necessary to point out that *output control* is one of the major weapons in the arsenal of the work group in dealing with management. Particularly where an incentive plan is in operation, some managements admitted they were powerless to deal with a concerted slowdown. The group retains the prerogative of whether or not it will work at an "incentive pace." Penalties for such behavior are sometimes very difficult to impose.

Where there is an incentive system, it means that some workers are more enthusiastic about increasing the level of earnings of the group than are others. Similarly, "pace" decisions affect the group differentially. It would appear that the "gaffer" or crew chief in a glass blowing team, because of the challenge, interest, and difficulty of his work, prefers a steady pace, while less skilled members of the crew prefer the pacing pattern more typical of mass production workers: spurts, "to get ahead of the quota," and then relative quiet periods "to enjoy life awhile." [47]

The same kind of situation is noted in Horsfall and Arensberg's study of a shoe factory, where the roughers made it a practice to be sure that a certain allocation of work was followed because they were most affected.[48]

(3) Meeting or exceeding company output standards can have other consequences besides those that are purely physical or financial. Particularly where the operations involved are skilled, the crew chief may take personal satisfaction in achieving difficult production goals. This would be most in evidence in situations where he strongly identified with management. Even where such identification is not the motivating factor, the sense of craftsmanship, the desire to prove to himself and his associates that he has the requisite skills to "make out" on the job, are powerful incentives to many crew chiefs. These needs may not be shared, in fact are unlikely to be shared, by the lesser skilled crew members who have not acquired that consciousness of craft. Thus conflicts over the importance of meeting standards develop between the higher skilled and lesser skilled members of work crews.

We have seen serious internal problems arise over just such issues. Very often the members of a crew are incensed to find that their leader has agreed with management to meet a certain output quota, without first consulting them.

(4) Needless to say, the two or more groups whose product meets at a point of blind coordination find it most difficult to achieve agreement on production levels. In our previous descriptions of such groups we noted that many of the frictions which preceded blowups were over this matter of output quantity, particularly over the pacing of work through the day.

To repeat, for the members of a crew, decisions regarding mutually approved rates of output are very critical because individual devia-

[47] These comments are based on discussions with Professors William F. Whyte and Frank Miller of Cornell University.

[48] Horsfall and Arensberg, *op. cit.*, p. 16.

tion is literally impossible, or almost so. However there are a number of factors present in many interdependent work situations which militate against easy agreement for these groups in their decision-making process.

Thus there is a basic paradox in the interdependent work departments which we observed. In terms of interaction and worker expectations, they were tightly knit social groups, but in many instances the social unit did not correspond with the economic unit. The social group was the crew, while frequently the economic group was the department comprised of many crews. In the case of the assembly line, the social group was often limited to a pair of employees or several overlapping pairs, while the economic group consisted of the entire line. Even within the boundaries of the social-economic group there were multiple sources of friction over rates of pay, output, and pacing. Therefore, as interest groups the interdependent work areas tended to be more divided and therefore weaker than work groups composed of autonomous employees.

Added to such conflict, of course, is the more apparent problem of the complex social structure of these groups and the requisite of intimate interworker coordination of effort. These factors, it might be expected, would be fertile grounds for interpersonal friction. The problem of getting along is magnified in the closely knit family, in part, because the family is such a close grouping and because the family is *expected* to get along. Each such dispute is grounds for guilt feeling. The inability to live up to the standard of perfect unity can be as personally frustrating as the cause of the friction itself. The cliché that family feuds are most fierce of all can appropriately be applied to the work team. Certainly supervisors have reported more interpersonal frictions in these settings than in areas of the plant where individual operations predominate.

While such events would preclude consistent, united action against management or the union, they would not preclude the periodic blowup directed against management or the union. The sudden wildcat strike over a minor disciplinary penalty assessed against a fellow worker may well be a reflection of such forces. We have already noted that in blind coordination points between mutually dependent operations, incidents involving high interpersonal friction are followed by aggressive actions against management. Management may be deceived by such occasional acts of solidarity toward external objects, which are, however, motivated by internal disunity (and often internal disloyalty).

A recent study of dockworker attitudes in Great Britain attributes some of the informal, irresponsible strike action characteristic of longshoring to just such kind of compensatory behavior:

> The satisfaction (the dockers) get from a public display of solidarity, particularly in support of a colleague who they think has been victimized, may, indeed, be due to the fact that such action helps them to get rid of the feelings of guilt aroused by selfish struggles among themselves (in securing good jobs).[49]

IMPACT OF INTERNAL SOCIAL LIFE ON PARTICIPATION IN OUTSIDE ACTIVITIES

There is some evidence in our study, although certainly not conclusive, that departments in which men work together on a crew or assembly basis are less likely to participate as groups in the life of the union than departments in which men are engaged in more individual activities. Pressmen (working as crews) participate less than typographers (working on individual jobs).[50] In the steel mills observed, rolling mill, hammershop, and furnace crews were less active than wire drawers (operating single machines). The "underground" and "overhead" departments (crew operations involving laying and maintenance of utility lines) in a large utility plant showed less participation than did the substation operators (an individual job) or the meter readers.[51] The British study of dock workers concludes:

> As it was also discovered that few "top six" men (dockers who consistently work together as a crew with the same supervisor) become informal leaders or are regular attenders at trade union and mass open-air meetings, it could only be concluded that the more the dock worker establishes permanent and satisfactory relationships with colleagues at work, the less he is prepared to take part in union activities.[52]

We would tend to modify the above conclusion for factory workers who do not typically enjoy the same "casual" status, characteristic of longshoring. The differences in the extent of on-the-job social relations in the factory among various groups are much more modest or subtle than the differences in social relations between the consistent crew members and the floaters and drifters on the docks. In the factory all employees share a much more integrated and persistent social life. The worker sees, talks with, and lives with a fairly limited number of fellow employees over a relatively long period, the

[49] University of Liverpool, Department of Social Science, *The Dock Workers*, The University Press of Liverpool, Liverpool, England, 1954, p. 67.

[50] Cf. Seymour Lipset, "Democracy in Private Government," *British Journal of Sociology*, III, 1952, p. 56.

[51] Personal communication from George Strauss.

[52] University of Liverpool, *op. cit.*, p. 72.

continuity being broken only by transfer, promotion, and the like. In her study of industrial unions, Dean finds, for example, that the better "integrated" employees (with senior status and, more satisfied than their fellows with work place and work associates, both in and out of the plant) are relatively *high participants* in the unions, but that the less well integrated employees are not.[53]

This difference in degree of integration or acceptance in the plant is not the same thing as the difference between crew membership and membership in individual operation departments. A crew member and a machine tender can be equally well integrated in the plant. However, the social demands on the crew members throughout the working day are much heavier than for their colleagues who work independently. The crew member is more restricted in adjusting his periods of social interaction and isolation to suit his moods, nor can he conveniently choose among those in the department with whom he wishes to maximize his interaction.[54] The job determines these things for him to a considerable extent; he is committed to a given small group for the major portion of his working time. We have no evidence that friendships are stronger or work groups more sociometrically matched in crew operations as compared to non-crew operations. In fact, there is some likelihood that the existence of status differences within the group and job-created frictions tend to militate against a high degree of internal unity.[55]

Argyris explains the lack of any significant informal group life on the part of certain bank employees (e.g., tellers) as attributable to the high frequency of interaction with customers required by the job. They are less likely to seek social satisfactions at the workplace than their fellow workers in departments that do not deal with the public:

[53] Lois R. Dean, "Social Integration, Attitudes and Union Activity," *Industrial and Labor Relations Review*, VIII, 1954, p. 58.

[54] Although, as noted on page 75, the evidence is not clear cut on this point.

[55] Sayles and Strauss, *op. cit.*, pp. 201, 205, 206. Stanley Seashore of the Survey Research Center of the University of Michigan supplied us with the raw data derived from one of the Center's studies of a heavy equipment manufacturing company. One of the variables they measured was the confidence workers placed in their fellow employees. The data were broken down by departments, and while our identification of independent and interdependent operations was not perfect, a preliminary sampling of departments where individual jobs predominated, showed these groups to be significantly *higher* in attitudinal variables related to confidence in fellow work group members than employees in crew and assembly operations. It should be noted that these findings are only suggestive, as we did not control the data for such factors as age, seniority, and status of the job.

Clearly, the most frequent interactions are between employee and customer.

As in the case of Department A (Trust Department) the human quality of these interactions helps the tellers to find adequate opportunity for personality expression. . . . These factors (customer interaction and lack of pressure from officers), in turn, account for the fact that employees tend to find little need for creating informal adaptive activities among themselves.

Since, as we have already pointed out, the employees are tied to the customer, and since the informal group activities do not exist, there results a work environment in which the employees hardly ever interact with each other.[56]

We conclude that a member of a production crew or assembly line is not prone to seek voluntarily many additional social commitments outside his immediate working groups. In terms of interacting with fellow workers, his job is more demanding than those of his non-crew colleagues in the plant. On the assumption that each individual has some total quantity of social interaction which represents a desired norm or equilibrium for him, the crew member is less likely to accept the union as his active responsibility.[57]

Low participation on the part of crew members may also be a reflection of their antipathy to the union. Such a consistent dislike among crews per se is somewhat difficult to accept unless:

(1) They are more likely to be skilled, and see less need for support from an industrial union.

(2) Because they themselves are ineffectual, and feel that the union is at fault for not doing more for them.

To be sure, there will be individual crew members who will be active in the union, but there will be fewer of them in relation to their total number than from the non-crew units. Those who do participate are likely to be seeking leadership positions, reflecting the same needs they demonstrated by advancing to positions such as crew chief.

What is the relation between participation and militance? Would a group that is less inclined to participate in the social-political life of a union, be less likely to file grievances or participate in a strike? The answer is a partial yes. The data show that grievance activity and union participation are related. This fact could be explained on the

[56] Chris Argyris, *Organization of a Bank,* Labor Management Center, Yale University, New Haven, Conn., 1954, p. 129.

[57] Cf. Eliot D. Chapple and Conrad M. Arensberg, *Measuring Human Relations,* Genetic Psychology Monographs, Vol. 22, 1940.

basis of our knowledge of the way the grievance procedure functions: in order to win cases, there must be constant pressure on union officials; friendly leaders (preferably from one's own department) must be selected; there must be occasional mass attendance at meetings and elections, petitions, etc.[58] Major grievances, that is, those requiring extended periods to process, demand a continuing, close association between union officialdom and the rank and file involved. This ability to work together many crew departments cannot provide.

On the other hand, the incidence of strike activity and other forms of explosive reaction to group problems do not have the same pattern of distribution as union participation by work group. Erratic behavior seems more likely to occur in interdependent work groups. This fact can be explained on the basis of the group's inexperience with, or inability to support, extended grievance activity. Failure to adapt to and function within the realities of the complaint system often leaves them no recourse but an aggressive display of force. But these groups also have poor participation records in their union.

Of course, contributing to their behavior is the lack of department-wide unity already referred to: the separateness of the crews and, where several job skills are combined, the divisions that exist within the crew itself.

Another way of viewing the impact of work-determined interaction on concerted self-interest activity is to look at two sharply contrasting situations. Many of the Conservative groups we have called scatter groups because the employees have such random-on-the-job contacts. These men are the maintenance workers, inspectors, in-plant truckers, and the members of some of the occupational groups we found in public utility operations.

What contacts they have are almost entirely social, rather than work-dominated. The work team as such hardly exists. When they meet at some central dispatching office, lunch room, or a chance spot in the plant, they are not overwhelmed by the petty problems of the immediate job. They can immediately begin appraising overall occupational problems and working conditions just because they do not see one another every hour of every day. Working conditions are not taken for granted.

In addition, this independence discourages the formation of small cliques based on job interaction. Such cliques are not readily ab-

[58] Leonard R. Sayles and George Strauss, "Some Problems of Communication in the Local Union," *Proceedings of the Fifth Annual Meeting of the Industrial Relations Research Association*, edited by L. Reed Tripp, Industrial Relations Research Association, Madison, Wis., 1953, pp. 143–149.

sorbed in larger action units. Men who share work intimately develop close ties on the job. Where there are a number of such small, tightly knit primary groups, an all-embracing economic pressure group may have problems in achieving overall consensus and loyalty.

IMPACT OF WORK FLOW ON GROUP LEADERSHIP

It should be observed that work crews that are not homogeneous, that have a number of skills included within the team, usually have a *functional leader*, a workman whose job description includes some responsibility for initiating and maintaining the work process. In fact, he is often referred to as the "crew chief" or "straw boss." A study by a colleague has presented an excellent summary of the problems of "role conflict" inherent in such a position.[59] In many ways the crew chief is caught "in the middle" like the foreman himself. His men pressure on one side and the supervisor on the other.

In the non-interdependent work situation the work group is somewhat freer to select whomever they wish for a position of informal leadership. Restricted only by the factor of size, which limits the available candidates, they can choose among those candidates whose personality and ability most clearly meet the needs of the position.

In the case of individual operations, the setup man may have responsibilities somewhat comparable to the crew chief. However, his primary contact with members of the group is at the start of each run and when he makes adjustments in the equipment when trouble arises. Although many job setters, because of seniority and skills, had the respect of fellow workers, who heeded their counsel, there was no evidence that they were selected more often than the operators for positions of informal leadership. Unlike the crew chief, they were not as intimately involved in the continuing operation; they did not initiate action for the other men as frequently as the operators initiated action for the setup man (by calling him to adjust their machines).

Although the crew chief does not have to be selected (or accepted) as informal leader, the work crews we observed had great difficulty in rejecting him. His influence was substantial because management and the union turned to him in order to deal with the group. Any attempt to establish a competing titular head caused strife within the group.

To be sure, many crew chiefs were ineffective and disliked as leaders. Their leadership was often rejected in favor of a secondary

[59] George Strauss, "The Set-up Man: A Case Study of Organizational Change," *Human Organization,* XIII, 1954, pp. 17–25.

figure. However, the rejection was never complete. The leadership within the group then was split.

How Many Leaders to a Group? There is no intention in this study to give an impression that the informal leadership of a work group is concentrated in one role. Indeed, a number of studies of work group activities indicate that informal leadership is diffused. One or two men will be responsible for initiating grievances. Behind the scenes others will serve to crystallize opinion and still others to adjust relationships within the group itself.[60]

There may also be real advantages to the group itself in this diffusion of the leadership role. Many of the leader's decisions for external affairs may be unpopular among a minority of the group. Particularly when there are differences within the group pertaining to age, sex, experience, and skill, complete concurrence on demands to be made to management and the union is unlikely. However, since a part of the high command may be unsullied by these necessary "discriminations," they help hold the group together.

In the case of work crews, diffusion of leadership is more difficult. The crew chief is such a dominant figure in the life of the group that others cannot compete with him easily, even on the basis of a division of the leadership function.

For example, it is interesting to note that work crews often select fairly low status members of the group to be stewards, when the chief himself does not assume that job (and when he does, there can be serious conflicts of interest, because the crew chief is a quasi-management official who is responsible for maintaining quality and quantity in production). Lacking any substantial prestige, the steward in such departments is more likely to be merely a figurehead as compared to the more important stewards in non-crew departments.

Crew chiefs vary in their approach to their leadership positions. Some try to maximize their superordinate position. They are proud to be known as stern autocrats. Such autocratic characteristics will be accepted by younger crew members, particularly in crews where there is an element of monopolized skill, that is, where the young men must depend on the good will of older, more skilled members for instruction and job information and the crew chief himself is a highly skilled craftsman. Often the chief decides for the men how much they will produce per hour, what rates they will demand from management, and many other questions as well. In one sense they are

[60] Cf. T. T. Paterson, *Morale in War and Work,* Max Parrish, London, 1955, pp. 123–126.

the direct descendents of those crew chiefs of an earlier age who acted as subcontractors. It will be recalled that management paid the subcontractor directly on a per piece basis, and that he in turn hired assistants and paid them out of his total earnings.

Many chiefs who lack the necessary job skills or an imposing personality attempt to fulfill an autocratic leadership role without success. They are then the subject of ridicule by fellow workers. The result is disadvantageous to the interests of the group itself, however, which consequently lacks an effective leader.

Reacting to a trend against authoritarianism (perhaps accompanied by a trend in favor of promotion within the crew on the basis of seniority rather than because of the approval of the crew chief), some crew chiefs and straw bosses minimize their decision-making powers. They attempt to limit themselves to those technical areas that are their particular province of expertise, leaving to the group itself the making of "value" decisions on what should be the group's policy toward the incentive system, working conditions, new members, and other matters of group-wide interest.

Many apparently are adopting a middle road, retaining their leadership position but consulting with fellow members and being guided by the consensus.[61]

However, the position of the crew chief or crew boss at best is a most difficult one. This in turn is reflected in the inability of the group to achieve the same integrated leadership that is possible in the work area having no job hierarchy or formally imposed straw boss.

COMPARING INTERDEPENDENT AND INDIVIDUAL WORK OPERATIONS

The work crew and short assembly line each has a greater need for internal unity than does the aggregation of employees who perform their work independently. The technologically interdependent members must come to a mutually acceptable decision concerning pace of work and total output. While the high frequency of their interaction causes them to become a tightly knit work team and social organization, the conflicting needs of the several included occupations and status levels can tend to destroy comparable unity in taking concerted action to attain work group goals. In addition, in departments which contain a number of similar crews or assembly groups, unity among them for common goals is made difficult by the self-enclosed

[61] This tendency is also reflected in material supplied by Whyte and Miller at Cornell.

character of each of the component units. Similarly, these groups are not free to select and change their leadership; the functional work leader selected for them tends to dominate the situation.

We would therefore expect, and do in fact find, that the members of work crews or of short assembly lines are not prone to engage in prolonged, carefully planned concerted activity on their own behalf. They lack clear-cut external goals of self-improvement. In part, this lack may be due to the richness of their internal promotional ladder (moving up to the level of crew chief), and to the fact that they have less need for, or less tolerance of, participation in such outside groups as the union. More tolerant of (or more used to) autocratic leadership, they countenance their own leaders acting as straw bosses and, in many situations, filling in as first line supervisors during the temporary absences of foremen, a dual responsibility that normally would not be permitted in groups comprised of technologically independent workers.

Crews and assembly groups may be involved in such demonstrations as wildcat strikes to a greater extent than other groups. Such strikes are certainly not a regular occurrence, but frustrations may build up in a group that has not established a systematic means of expressing discontent. Although groups of employees who individually control their work may overdo the expression of grievances, this activeness means at least that their problems do not become cumulative. The crew or short assembly line may appear to be relatively well satisfied over a long period, but then a sudden explosion occurs, and the men engage in a serious walkout.[62] We shall turn to this problem again in the next chapter.

The same conclusions obviously do not hold for the homogeneous crew, which does not have problems of complex structure and leader-

[62] A contrary explanation is offered by Gouldner in his study of a gypsum board plant and the associated mining operation. In contrasting the attitudes and behavior of the miners with the more typical factory workers employed on "surface" operations, he finds that the miners who worked in closely knit small crews did *not* engage in carefully premeditated, drawn-out pressure activities because: "(They) tended to allow themselves more ready expression of open aggression . . . (They) were more capable of expressing disagreements with or aggression toward authority."

Their spontaneity and outbursts were the result of a readiness to scorn supervision, to reject the authority system of the organization. However, it should be noted, as Gouldner well describes, that the unique environmental conditions present in mining, that is, the constant danger, the traditions of the craft, and the type of person attracted, contribute a great deal to the characteristic patterns of miner-employer relations. Alvin W. Gouldner, *Patterns of Industrial Bureaucracy*, Free Press, Glencoe, Ill., 1954, p. 136.,

ship. By definition, its members have a maximum of common interests. The resonance factor in such groups is magnified, and they show high concerted activity. But their basic instability and inability to restrain immediate action probably makes them incapable of the calculated and basically important long-run kinds of demands which are characteristics of Strategic groups. They have a "handicap"—because of the close, family-like relationships fostered within the crew, it is difficult for them to form combinations into larger department units, which are more appropriate for the handling of many problems.

Interdependent work operations maintain a delicate internal balance; new members can "quickly sour the whole bunch," in the words of several management officials. It is more difficult to incorporate a new member because of the coordination required by the process, but at the same time it is easier for the neophyte to extend his influence once he is accepted. For this reason too, we have come to expect rapid *spontaneous conversions* from these groups, such as, shifts from low output to high output, no grievances to many grievances, or docility to a wildcat walkout. Communications are almost immediate, reinforced by the completely shared experiences of the entire group. Thus, a really embittered employee can have a startling effect on fellow worker attitudes and behavior in such groups, as can a highly satisfied worker with leadership potential.

Summary

In Section A of this chapter we concluded that a group of factors affecting the status of the work group and its included occupations —in relation to other groups in the plant—affected their level of grievance activity. On the other hand, the *quality of the pressures* exerted by such interest groups is affected, to a substantial degree, by the *internal organization of the work unit,* as determined, primarily, by the work flow and division of labor. Interdependence in the work process tends to be associated with the more spontaneous, sporadic kinds of outbursts. Sustained activity, which seems to be the product of carefully thought-through, long-run objectives, is more characteristic of independent, individual operations than of crew and assembly lines. Homogeneous crews have long records of grievances, slowdowns, and all the rest, but the volume of the outburst bears little relation to the perception of inequity or the importance of the goal to be attained.

A group whose members perform interdependent operations has the following handicaps, which make continuous, deliberate pressure activities more difficult for them:

1. Where job skills are mixed in the group, status and interest differences militate against concerted action.
2. Internal promotion ladders often reduce the widespread dissatisfaction associated with aggregations of employees in the same job classification, who have "no place to go" in terms of realistic advancement possibilities.
3. The interaction pattern flowing from the engineering arrangement of jobs often stimulates the formation of small cliques that do not readily combine into larger action units. The arrangement may not stimulate identification of the social group with the work unit. As a result, work frictions arise which stimulate flare-ups that we would classify as Erratic.
4. Internal differences over output control are likely in these kinds of groups, further sapping the strength of the group.
5. There is some evidence that workers whose jobs require relatively continuous intercommunication and interaction are less likely to participate in self-interest activities, such as union processes, which require still further interpersonal contacts.
6. Work crews are often saddled with a formally designated leader (the crew chief), who retains substantial influence on the members although he is ineffectual, from their point of view, in providing a unifying type of leadership.

We observed that many work areas which are technologically closely knit give rise to an internal quarrelsomeness that is likely to extend outside to management and the union. While troublesome and often seemingly irrational, they pose much shorter-lived problems than those originating in groups characterized by Strategic behavior.

Considering both the intergroup and intragroup variables we found the following relations:

I Consistently high grievance and other pressure activities (Erratic and Strategic Groups)

Associated with: Middle to high range of jobs
Worker control over job performance
Indispensable operators
High similarity of economic interests

II Spontaneous, unpredictable grievance and pressure activity (Erratic and Apathetic Groups)

Associated with: Groups whose members performed inter-dependent operations—crews and assembly lines
Breaks and imperfections in work flow

III Deliberate, predictable grievance and pressure activity (Strategic and Conservative Groups)

Associated with: Operations performed by members individually and independently, and, on occasion, short, homogeneous assembly lines and homogeneous crews

IV Low, intermittent grievance and pressure activity (Apathetic and Conservative Groups)

Associated with: Very high or very low status jobs

SIGNIFICANCE OF TECHNOLOGY

Thus, if we were looking at the organization chart and work flow (layout) of an industrial plant, certain predictions could be made with some confidence regarding the behavior of work groups. If some concentrations of jobs had certain characteristics, they would probably be centers of industrial relations problems; other characteristics would cause us to predict the absence of such frictions.

Upon reflection it appears as though all of our relevant variables are related to the technological system designed by the company to organize the work process. The degree of independence or dependence among workers in the flow of work, the number and similarity of jobs concentrated in any one location, the indispensability of any part to the whole, the extent to which work loads and output standards can be accurately defined, and even the promotional ladders (and status relationships) are determined to a large extent by the kinds and quantity of equipment, skills, and plant layout utilized.

We recognize that many persistent industrial relations problems have their roots in the technology of the plant. We are in the habit of attributing these to individual worker and manager characteristics and to the quality of the working environment. We say that these problems tend to continue because the jobs are unpleasant, repetitive, mechanically paced, heavy or dirty, or that they are exacting in terms of the quantity and quality of output required. However, this study suggests that the social system erected by the technological process is also a basic and continuing determinant of work group attitudes and actions.

Differences in the structure of such groups, in addition to the members' satisfactions and dissatisfactions with specific environmental conditions, are significant variables which shape the collective behavior of the members.

chapter **4**

Dynamics of work group behavior

To this point our analysis of group behavior in the plant and its causes has been a static one. We have identified four relatively distinctive behavior patterns and have attempted to relate them to job configurations. But these technological factors are really *enabling conditions.* They do not explain what sets off a spate of aggressive activity, what brings it to a halt, and what are the personal motivations involved. It is these dynamic problems which are the subject of this chapter. They are the intervening variables between organizational structure and group action.

Our first approach to the questions above is an examination of some of the similarities among various behavior types. As we shall see, these comparisons suggest sharp differences in motivation between the Apathetic and Erratic groups on one hand, and the Strategic and Conservative ones on the other. Also, the qualities of internal leadership they find acceptable differ significantly.

Secondly, shifts in the behavior that the groups exhibit over a period of time reveal many of the underlying forces shaping the decisions of group members. These shifts are the deviant cases that are exceptions to our general finding that behavior patterns are stable over relatively long periods. Such unexpected and often drastic changes, as in the case of all periods of transition, are enlightening for the observer.

After summarizing our conclusions on the motivations of these groups and on the relation between their own conception of their relative power and their grievance activity, job behavior, and selection of leadership, we turn to some consideration of the plant as a single entity. Not unexpectedly, it would appear that the total overall industrial relations climate of the plant is a function of the kinds of work groups included.

Our objective is to move from the fine detail of the earlier chapters to larger patterns of behavior. This procedure will enable us, in succeeding chapters, to consider the implication of these configurations for management, for the union, and for research on work groups in industry.

Similarities and Differences in Group Types

We have observed that there are persistent differences among work groups in their tendency to challenge management decisions (and often union decisions as well). More important, these differences are represented in tangible variations in the intensity and number of protest actions of one kind or another, actions which are, to an extent, apparently independent of management and union personnel and their policies.

Thus we have classified some of the work groups reported as relatively inactive; these we called our Apathetic and Conservative types. Others, which we said were the consistent hot spots or tension areas of the plants surveyed, we termed the Erratic and Strategic groups. Interestingly, however, the dividing line most sharply defined by the data is not the one separating the highly active self-interest groups from the relatively inactive, passive ones. It is the behavior patterns of the Apathetic and Erratic groups which basically are similar. In parallel, the behavior patterns of the Strategic and the Conservative groups also have much in common.

THE BEHAVIOR OF THE APATHETIC-ERRATIC AXIS

The groups whose behavior places them in the Apathetic-Erratic categories seem much more *personal* in their relationship with management and the union. They are not seeking any long-run readjustments in their relative economic and prestige position in the plant. Rather, they usually are attempting to preserve their customary rights. Theirs is a holding operation, usually much less involved with the use of the union as a pressuring agent than other more "far-seeing" work groups.

Because the expectations of the Apathetic-Erratic groups are often not made explicit, compared to the insistent demands of the more premeditative groups (Strategic and Conservative), their reactions to management moves are often unpredictable. Further, such reactions are likely to be the product of real frustration. There is a high emotional content in their dependence upon customary relations with supervision and their desire to preserve the status quo. When these conditions are "violated," the reaction can be sudden and violent. When the members of these groups are convinced that their "way of life" is threatened they will fight back as savagely, if not more so, as the group that in a calculating way is seeking some new benefit or right.

This need to preserve customary relations is difficult to make explicit. The protests of these groups seldom center on specific overt violations of contractual agreements, or if they do, their real causes are not recognized by management and the union. Therefore, such grievances may continue and grow, and when the break comes it is more likely to be sudden and explosive because of pent-up dissatisfaction. The grievance procedure, whatever its structure, has failed to drain off the frustrations. Often there will be an element of contagion throughout the process, the overt expression of dissatisfaction spreading among those most susceptible to it.

The following case may serve as an example of the kind of behavior to which we refer:

> Department X had been complaining for many months that they were receiving less per hour for certain work than another department which periodically handled similar jobs. They hounded their grievance man but never submitted a formal grievance. One particular day, for no apparent reason the men got together and signed a petition which stated that they wanted an immediate meeting with the company, and would refuse to work until something was done about their wages. Management refused to meet with them, insisting that their rates were correct as stipulated in the contract. A meeting with local union officials and the staff representative of the international union was finally arranged for later that day. At the afternoon meeting, the men were told that the union was also concerned with the matter and would attempt to eliminate the inequity in the forthcoming contract negotiations. The men went back to work, and the sudden flurry of activity came to a halt. It was the last the union heard from that particular group, even though the matter was not brought up during the subsequent negotiations.
>
> To recapitulate: With no advance notice to the union the men

threatened a strike unless their demands were met. The "petition" seemed to be a sudden impulse, and when it failed to budge management or the union, the men went back to their jobs. In many similar instances, an actual walkout or sit-down takes place, with just about as much foreplanning and chance for success. The resulting stoppage is embarrassing to the union as well as to management.

The groups which lack the cohesion required for careful advance planning and the patience born of bargaining skill often find themselves in a box of their own making. They rashly commit themselves to abrupt and illegal action; then when management or the union threatens reprisals, they have no organizational means to back down and still save face. Thus many of their aggressive activities may be the result of the frustration created by their own actions, which have closed all acceptable retreats or means of escape.

Paradoxically, the most discouraging aspect of the position of the Apathetic and Erratic groups in the plant is the likelihood that they will provide the most serious opposition to technological change. Although the Apathetics offer minimum open challenges to management, their attitude, as well as that of the Erratics, is a blind resistance to what is new and different. They lack the internal organization and structure which would provide them with the capacity for change. To be sure, innovation can be imposed upon them, but as individuals they remain convinced that they have been seriously injured and the results will be calamitous. Thus their output often suffers for extended periods, not because of a concerted slowdown, but because the individual employee is sure that his job has been made much more difficult, and unfairly so.[1]

THE BEHAVIOR OF THE CONSERVATIVE-STRATEGIC AXIS

In contrast to the behavior described above, we have seen that many work groups are more legalistically inclined. They have learned, particularly since the advent of the union, to think in contract terms, and they are ever ready to check management's conformity with the literal meaning of that document. If we were to surmise their mental processes, we might envision a continuously functioning computer working out the ratio:

[1] For a good example of this type of resistance to change see the description by French and Coch of the long period required to get pieceworkers in a men's wear factory to adjust their output back to normal after minor work changes were introduced by management. Lester Coch and John R. P. French, Jr., "Overcoming Resistance to Change," *Human Relations*, I, 1948.

$$\frac{\text{Our Importance in the Plant}}{\text{Any Other Group's Importance}} = \frac{\text{Our Earnings}}{\text{Their Earnings}}$$

At times they are satisfied, being assured by the computation that they are doing "all right." But more often, particularly for those groups in the middle that we have called Strategic, the old doubts remain that "we are not getting all to which we are entitled." As long as these doubts continue, pressure will be applied at every conceivable opportunity which promises the chance of getting more for themselves.

Most of their legalistic grievances are well thought through and well expressed. There is little likelihood of sudden explosion, because both management and the members understand their demands. Their very ability to communicate these wants increases the chance of their being satisfied or, put in another way, decreases the possibility of any sudden explosion. Management can predict with a fair degree of accuracy when the mild pressures of these groups will be purposefully converted into more serious concerted demonstrations.

In turn, because they can be bargained with, agreement on the introduction of change in the groups can be more readily, although not painlessly, obtained. Theirs is not blind resistance to innovation. Therefore, when "sold," they will completely adopt and adapt to the new circumstances rather than engage in either extended passive resistance or pitched battles.

Another way of looking at this basic distinction between the Erratic-Apathetic groups on the one hand and the Strategic-Conservative groups on the other is suggested by Gouldner in his report on a wildcat strike. He contrasts "the 'traditionalists' who were custom rooted (and) sought a restoration of the past . . . with the 'market men' who sought formal recognition of *new* rights and obligations . . . (and) emphasized the pecuniary implications of workers' grievances . . ."[2]

His intensive analysis of a single plant appears to be consistent with the findings of this study.

VARIATIONS IN TYPE OF INFORMAL LEADER SELECTED

In an important sense, the leadership qualities of the informal leader (or on occasion the union official), through whom the interest group deals with management and union are the crucial link between potential action and action taken. The leader does not himself deter-

[2] Alvin W. Gouldner, *Wildcat Strike*, The Antioch Press, Yellow Springs, Ohio, 1954, pp. 61–62.

mine the actions of his group; the group will tend to select an individual whose characteristics suit their unique temperament. Our data in this area are only suggestive, since we had little contact with these men and descriptions of their behavior were highly incomplete. It would appear, however, that there is a significant relationship between the personality type that appeals to a group and the kind of group involved.[3]

Apathetic groups and, to a lesser extent, Erratic groups frequently seemed to permit the leadership function to gravitate to highly aggressive individuals with a strong need to dominate the situation, both within the group and in group relations with management and the union. These individuals would tolerate no competition for the center of the stage; they had to have the last word in every encounter. Most interesting, and certainly most unexpected from the point of view of many management officials, was the readiness with which these leaders could on occasion transfer their censorious focus from the company to the rank and file. Even while describing their role in precipitating a wildcat strike or a serious verbal attack on the company, they might comment that the company was making a mistake in not promoting them into the personnel department! Needless to say, their belief that such staff men have the authority to impose their point of view on the employees makes it seem clear that theirs was not a rebellion against authority but, rather, a highly aggressive need to demonstrate authority and to work within an authoritarian framework.

The social scientist might describe these kinds of people as "charismatic" leaders. Their striking and appealing personality characteristics, the uniqueness which sets them apart from their colleagues, makes them the obvious choice of those groups that wish to be dominated, or better, wish to follow a "spellbinder."

In contrast it would appear that Strategic and Conservative groups selected individuals who temperamentally were much more suited to responding to the initiations of the group. The group, being able to demonstrate a consensus toward problems, utilized as an external leader someone who would do their bidding and would not go off on his own. In fact they would reject the leadership attempts of members within their own groups whom they considered overbearing, irresponsible, or dangerous.

Such leaders were much less flashy. Although they might be intellectually committed to an antimanagement bias and determined to press certain grievances with all the vigor they possessed, they did

[3] Also see previous chapter, section entitled, "How Many Leaders to a Group?" p. 88.

not seem to demonstrate aggressiveness for the sake of being aggressive. Their hostilities expressed themselves in controlled convictions, not emotional outbursts. As such, they were much easier to negotiate with, and when one such leader was promoted to a management position he was likely to do a good job of supervision. This situation contrasted with the showing of the charismatic leaders developed in Apathetic and Erratic groups, who, after appointment to supervisory positions, often incurred the enmity of employees because of their autocratic approach to the job of managing.

SHIFTS IN GROUP BEHAVIOR OVER TIME

Our analysis to this point has been concerned with the static elements in work group behavior. We have been primarily interested in examining group behavior and in turn relating it to plant technology.

Actually we have already departed to some extent from this static picture by describing two kinds of cases where relatively short-run shifts take place. We observed a number of instances when Erratic groups shifted dramatically to Apathetic, in almost miraculous "conversions." Overnight, sometimes, a contentious trouble spot became cooperative and peaceful. This event might often be related to a change in the elected steward, to management action, or to unknown internal changes. What was significant about the conversions, however, was the rapidity with which they took place, seemingly much faster than any basic morale change could work itself out. Just as quickly such a group might shift back to the offensive, and with no greater provocation than had previously occurred.

Although we have no definite evidence on this possibility, it is likely that the susceptibility of these groups to the influence of a stranger, to which we referred earlier, may be partially responsible for the conversion phenomenon. A newly introduced troublemaker or a newly elected steward who believes in a more disciplined department can affect the group with unusual swiftness.

Similarly in the case of Conservative groups, we noted several instances where previous inactivity had placed them at a disadvantage in the scale of plant benefits. For a short period they then responded like Strategic groups, charging forward simultaneously on many fronts to pressure management to make concessions. When the battle was won, however, they usually returned to their former inactive status. Nevertheless, their conversions were not the sudden shifts characteristic of Erratic groups, but rather the result of a gradual recognition that they had fallen behind in plant benefits.

Let us now examine two longer-run shifts.

TWO CASES OF A SHIFT TO DECREASED ACTIVITY

(1) We observed a group of grinder operators who, over a period of some years, had been one of the most successfully active groups in a large steel plant. The men had elected a number of top union officials; they had won a desirable incentive plan, and they were noted plant-wide for their excellent working conditions. However, management initiated technological changes which decreased the importance of their operation. These changes made it possible to complete at an earlier production step certain elements of their work. As a result of decreased work, a number of bitter internecine disputes over seniority problems broke out within the group, destroyed its unity for a number of years and eliminated any influence it had in plant affairs.[4]

Thus a typical Strategic-type group (with its concentration of individual, middle-rung machine operators) became an Apathetic one.

(2) A group of production broach operators had won nearly every objective they sought. They had the unchallenged leadership of the plant. Rarely have we observed such unanimity of opinion concerning the "best" job in the plant. Workers and management alike were convinced that these men had the most desirable jobs with the highest earnings. As a matter of fact, other occupational groups among the production workers often surpassed them in earnings, as did the toolroom, but plant opinion remained the same: "The broach operators are the highest!" Although they comprised only about 3 per cent of the plant work force, a series of union presidents had come from the department, and they had representatives in both factions that usually competed for elective positions in the union. Requests for improvement in their working conditions were usually met by swift management compliance. In reality, grievances were rare and concerted pressure only a memory.

Structurally, the group fits clearly into our Strategic category. Although the jobs are individual and have close tolerances, they are in no sense a skilled craft requiring a long training period. In this work a number of operators are concentrated in one geographic location, and they are replaceable; current broach operators cannot easily find similar work outside the plant. Yet the behavior of our group was typically that of a Conservative group. They were no longer

[4] This case is more fully reported in the author's, "A Case Study of Union Participation and Technological Change," *Human Organization*, II, 1952, pp. 5–15. In reality, the operation described was centerless grinding. The term "machine polishers" was used to prevent identification of the group during the period when some of these changes were still taking place.

pushing for new benefits, and legalistic grievances were a rarity. They had won an unambiguous position of secure respect and assured benefits, and were responding with true *noblesse oblige.*

Even though we think we can explain these two shifts, there remain a number of unresolved questions. The reader will recall the observation of union representative, that the metal polishers in one plant lost their strength when management scattered their operation among a number of departments. Yet we have observed many groups with substantial economic strength whose operations are scattered. However, the latter groups have not experienced any change; inspectors, for example, have always been located in widely separated locations.

In the automobile industry the trimmers have not suffered any apparent decrease in their ability to exert concerted pressure, although they suffered a serious technological blow when stapling and new materials rendered unnecessary some of their upholstering skills. Why did they not suffer the same fate as the grinders described above? One difference may be that the trimmers' change in the automobile industry did not result in decreased job opportunities for the men involved. Thus, their strength was not sapped by internal squabbles over who should retain job rights.

Explanations such as these are not satisfactory, however. We need to know much more about the conditions under which pressure groups change their behavior patterns. All we are able to do at this point in our research is to suggest which kinds of shifts are most likely to occur.

It would seem that additional research will disclose the following shifts to be somewhat common:

Temporary or Short Run	Reason
Erratic ⟶ Apathetic	Unknown (what we have called conversions)
Apathetic ⟶ Erratic	Unknown (what we have called conversions)
Conservative ⟶ Strategic	Group has fallen behind in terms of benefits

Long Run	Reason
Strategic ⟶ Apathetic	Loss of critical factor in relative plant position or unity
Strategic ⟶ Conservative	Permanent improvement in plant status

It should be noted that the short-run shifts take place within the two major constellations: Apathetic-Erratic and Strategic-Conservative, not between them.

Group Goals and Motivations

In most of our discussion up to this point we have been interested in examining persistent differences in group behavior rather than in explaining the motivation of the members responsible for any given pattern of action. To be sure, we have made reference to very general kinds of goals, such as the maintenance or improvement of economic benefit levels shared by the members of the interest group. However, such explanations are rather inadequate, particularly when we begin discussing the shifts undergone by some groups as described previously. At this stage, then, we want to summarize our knowledge of group goals. There is a direct interrelation between the plant environment and work group behavior that we can point to as having some significance in setting off certain chain reactions. At least three distinct influences on work group goals can be distinguished:

1. Intraplant comparisons of benefits one group enjoys to those others are receiving.
2. Some direct threat to security emanating usually, but not exclusively, from management.
3. As a function of the previous success or failure of the group in responding to 1 and/or 2.

Let us explore each of these factors briefly.

1. Intraplant Comparisons

We have already observed that high activity is associated with a somewhat ambiguous prestige position. Work groups in the upper middle ranges of skill and earnings have met some of the criteria which justifies in their eyes, if not in management's view, pay and working conditions "almost" comparable to those enjoyed by the recognized top skilled personnel. As we noted in the case of the hand screw machine operators, these middle-range workers expect to be much better off than those they see as being *below* them in importance, and almost as well off as those they recognize as being *above* them in job skills. They utilize the same reference groups to establish their skill level, seizing upon one criterion, such as the fineness of the tolerances for the work they are doing, and excluding others which do not support their case.

We have referred to special interest groups because these groups have particular economic goals: securing better work standards, greater protection in the case of technological change, higher hourly rates, more overtime, looser incentive standards, and so on. Each of the goals has a *comparative* aspect: better than, greater than, higher than, looser than, more than the conditions or status of some other group.

The plant grapevine carries general impressions as to how hard various groups work for approximately what general order of income —although the accuracy of these impressions leaves much to be desired. Actually we know very little about how these comparisons are made, and need to know much more before generalizing on how a group decides it is being paid equitably or inequitably.[5]

The economist has stressed interplant comparisons as the dynamic force in the labor market. We would suggest that with the impact of seniority, retirement, job guarantees, and the protections of unionization, the internal (to the firm) labor market becomes an equally important determinant of worker behavior.

An interesting example of the effect of "other work groups" was furnished by a steelworker official. He observed that foundries are often hot spots, highly aggressive in seeking fulfillment of their demands *when they are part of larger manufacturing organizations.* However, when the plant is entirely devoted to the foundry operation, they are relatively weak and inactive.

We might speculate that in these more diversified plants the position of the foundry is ambiguous. Earnings are high to compensate for the difficult working conditions, the work is heavy, and more recently there has been a serious shortage of applicants for this kind of work; but the reputation of the foundry is very low among other employees, who tend to look down on foundry workers because of the hot, dirty, heavy work they perform.

Our study of the decision-making process in local unions concluded that there are many areas subject to collective bargaining in which

[5] For evidence that proximity is an important factor in the comparisons made by these individuals, note the following observation: "The more distant the wage comparison—in level of wages, in work process or in geographical or departmental location—the less significant it is." Robert Livernash, "Job Evaluation," in *Employment and Wages in the United States,* edited by W. S. Woytinsky and associates, Twentieth Century Fund, New York, 1953, p. 431.

one group gains relatively more than another. There are other group demands which can only be satisfied at the direct expense of some other work group. For the former case a typical example is the negotiation of specific job rates:

Whenever the union officers obtain improved earnings for one group they reduce the relative prestige of other workers. The elimination of what are inequities in the eyes of one group may create inequities in the eyes of a competing department. . . . Whenever the union initiates or acquiesces to change affecting job evaluation or incentive rates it runs the risk of upsetting *customary differentials*.[6]

THE ECONOMIC WORLD OF THE WORKER
IN HIS WORK GROUP

Potential Promotion
Potential Promotion
Are these good jobs in our line of promotion?
near jobs
near jobs
near jobs
Are these higher paying jobs actually more skilled than our own?
OUR JOB
near jobs
near jobs
near jobs
Do we earn enough more than the lower rated jobs to compensate for the skill difference?
Potential Downgrade
Potential Downgrade
Are there suitable jobs below to fall back on if there are cutbacks?

Description: These are the types of intergroup comparisons that the employee constantly makes, particularly in a unionized plant.

[6] Leonard Sayles and George Strauss, *The Local Union*, Harper & Brothers, New York, 1953, pp. 45–46.

Then there are instances where one group must lose, in an absolute sense, if some other group is to gain its demands. Seniority issues, division of retroactive pay, and decisions where work within the plant is to be performed are relevant examples of the win-lose pattern.

In all of these examples one group is comparing its gains from unionization with the gains of another group. In fact, the introduction of the union often increases the importance of these rivalries:

> Before the union was organized, poor communications made it difficult for one group to compare itself with another. Information about weekly paychecks, hours worked, seniority, and all the rest could be passed from group to group only by means of rumors and personal friendships.
>
> The unions have opened new channels of communication. Contract requirements that seniority lists and job vacancies be posted create a wealth of opportunities for workers to compare their positions in the plant. Job evaluation rates all the jobs in the plant against *each other*. . . . Just as workers are now sensitive to cost-of-living indices, they know what the "other guys are getting and how hard they work for it." [7]

Finally, by providing a grievance procedure which channels worker complaints into areas where something can and often is done about them, the union encourages the development of intergroup comparisons. (See diagram on page 105.)

2. EXTERNAL THREAT

Secondly, a threat to a group's existing benefit level may stimulate the members to action. This is the motivation analyzed in much of the research on informal group behavior in industry. As deduced in the Western Electric studies, the behavior observed in the Bank Wiring Room was a reaction to the threat of management changes:

> The Bank Wiring Observation Room seemed to show that action taken in accordance with the technical organization tended to break up, through continual change, the routines and human associations which gave work its value. The behavior of the employees could be described as an effort to protect themselves against such changes, to give management the least possible opportunity of interfering with them. When they said that if they increased their output, "something" was likely to happen, a process of this sort was going on in their minds. But the process was not a conscious one. It is important to point out that the protective functioning of informal organization is not a product of deliberate planning. It was more in the nature of an automatic response. The curious thing is that, as Professor Mayo pointed out to the Committee, these informal organiza-

[7] *Ibid.*, p. 57.

tions much resemble formally organized labor unions, although the employees would not have recognized the fact.[8]

We have suggested that threats to the existing status quo are more important for Apathetic and Erratic groups which tend to react spontaneously than for the groups which are more legalistically oriented. However, even for the latter groups, some threat in the current situation may be the initial motivating factor to convert a potentially active group into a consistently aggressive one. As Caplow suggests, there may be an optimum level of threat (for example, a technological change that reduces the skill level necessary to perform a given kind of work) which "jells" the group into an action-oriented unit.[9] Tasting success, they remain active, although the original threat has disappeared. However, their goal is no longer a return to normalcy, but, rather, is directed toward improvement.

Perhaps there should be a special category called "obsolescence groups." Managements report that certain groups whose technological importance has declined drastically are never-ending sources of grievances. The trimmers whose skill with the tack hammer has been replaced by the use of stapling guns may be a good case in point. Certain foundry occupations similarly have lost their skill requirements and are focal points for trouble. (Of course, the economist may rightly call such group efforts unsuccessful if their militant demands encourage management to substitute machinery or new methods more rapidly than it would otherwise have done; but this judgment is not necessarily relevant to the group itself.)

Where the threat is too imposing, the result can be demoralization. As we have noted, there are many instances where reduced work opportunities resulted in serious internal bickerings over seniority and in differences with the union which destroyed an active group.

3. RELATIONS OF GROUP POWER TO ITS LEVEL OF ACTIVITY

By implication, at least, we have been talking about this third variable: How much does the level of aggressive activity depend on the inherent *power* residing within the group? We might easily assume that power which insures successful group efforts would en-

[8] George Homans, "The Western Electric Researches," in *Human Factors in Management,* edited by Schuyler D. Hoslett, Harper & Brothers, New York, 1951, p. 240.

[9] Theodore Caplow, *The Sociology of Work,* University of Minnesota Press, Minneapolis, 1954, p. 137.

courage still greater efforts. After pressuring for an easier work standard and winning it, we might expect to find further incentive to repeat this behavior. Surely the psychologists with their Law of Effect would predict: behavior that is rewarded tends to be repeated. A British economist has observed: "If there is one thing which can be more damaging to the orderly conduct of industrial relations than an unofficial strike, it is a successful unofficial strike." [10]

We know more about the negative situation; it is easier to observe. The failure of a group to achieve an objective, particularly when the failure can be attributed to internal faults in organization, reduces the incentive to try again.

One department sought to gain a premium payment for a holiday eve or, preferably, time off without pay when production quotas for the period had already been met. They noted that other departments did not have night work before a holiday. When management refused, the men agreed among themselves to stay home on the night concerned and then claim to have been ill. When the shift reported the following evening, half of the members learned that the other half had been on the job the previous night. After that fiasco, suggestions that the group try other pressure tactics, such as a slowdown to obtain a looser incentive standard, were always greeted with the same answer: "Yeah, look what happened last time—why would I risk my neck so that someone else can go behind my back and cut my throat for me?"

In another case reported by the author, the failure of just that kind of endeavor was instrumental in discouraging group efforts for some years. In that department, a number of senior workers ignored an agreement to turn in less production as a means of contesting new production standards.[11]

It would seem reasonable for a group to take into account its *chances for success* before pushing ahead with a protest. We expect that the group's "experience rating" of their own power would condition their protests of shop conditions. It has been suggested that groups that have experienced the effectiveness of their power are more likely to see "poor" working conditions, "tight" standards, "tough" supervision, etc., as correctable. Those that have experienced failure may see the same things as *inevitable* conditions in their kind of plant or industry, inherent and unchangeable.[12]

[10] K. G. J. C. Knowles, *Strikes—A Study in Industrial Conflict*, Blackwell & Mott, Oxford, England, 1952, p. 35.

[11] Sayles, *op. cit.*, pp. 8–9.

[12] Cf. Margaret Chandler's description of a plant where the workers had ex-

Of course, success breeds success in other ways as well. Members' attraction to a group, and the loyalty they are willing to demonstrate toward it (in terms of maintaining unity of purpose and undergoing sacrifices in common struggles) varies directly with the prestige accorded the group. When successes are forthcoming, the attachment becomes stronger. Conversely, failures weaken identification, and persistent failures may result in the individuals complete severance of all ties with his work group. We have observed instances where employees applied for transfers out of departments which they saw as lacking influence in plant affairs and suffering thereby. Many times key leaders and prestige figures are lost in the members' rush to find a safer haven within a group that is more powerful in defending its interests.

However, we have also seen that there may be an end, or at least a temporary halt to the spiral—success—new demands—more success, etc. Although we do not believe in the concept of the static equilibrium which, once reached, shuts off further demands, there are cases where a group places itself in such a preferred position that there is little incentive for further activity. A shift of behavior pattern from Strategic to Conservative would be an illustration. Such a transformation is probably due in part to management's own change of attitude concerning the group. The company learns to anticipate the probable reaction of employees before acting, thus "protecting" the group from hardship. This is more likely to be the case with respect to Conservative groups that have a high replacement value than to Strategic groups which often appear to be more expendable.

Finally, in this consideration of the relation between power and activity, we have observed that serious intragroup frictions (an element of weakness, not strength) may be a contributing cause of some serious outbursts against management because:

1. Under some circumstances, the members of the group may find it acceptable to express their frustrations over interpersonal frictions in antimanagement grievances. This action provides an aggressive outlet and also serves to assuage any feelings of guilt over their failure to be normal and to like one another as members of the same family.

---

perienced failure: "Their 'aggressions' against both management and the union largely consisted of informal 'griping' sessions. Moreover, much of the 'griping' took on a philosophical character, for there was always a note of, 'Oh, well, what can you do about it?' " *Labor-Management Relations in Illini City, Case Study 3: Garment Manufacture,* University of Illinois, Institute of Labor and Industrial Relations, Champaign, Ill., 1953 p. 473.

2. There will be times when internal differences make it impossible even to express a grievance that represents a consensus. The group is in disagreement, not agreement, over what needs "righting." As a result, the normal and peaceful workings of the grievance procedure do not drain off the problems. Rather, a substantial backlog of unsolved and often unexpressed dissatisfaction accumulates, until the inevitable explosion occurs.[13]

Here we have a rather fine distinction. Those unsuccessful in utilizing group pressures to win improved benefits for themselves are more likely to accept certain elements of their working life as inevitable, elements that the more successful groups might be willing to challenge. However, these same unsuccessful groups have a low level of tolerance for many petty threats from management. Lacking any assurance that they have enough control in the situation to win out eventually, they may explode, almost spontaneously—at times when they think they see an inequity coming.

On the other hand, where self-confidence has been built up over time with the recognition that "we do swing some weight around here," petty annoyances and fears can be tolerated. As we have noted, prolonged negotiations and pressure tactics require patience and restraint. Overt pressures must be saved for the more important cases.

This kind of conclusion is also suggested in a recent study of worker morale:

> We might, for example, think that a work group which had been accustomed to certain high levels of satisfaction would be more seriously threatened by a reduction in those levels than a group for which the level of satisfaction in the past had been lower or less reliable. This may not however be exactly the case. It is quite possible that the former group will prove to be more stable in tolerating present deprivations than the latter. It is not necessarily true that the way to learn frustration tolerance is to be frustrated.[14]

To summarize, we have presented some "motivational" reasons, aside from the structural elements relating to these work groups, that would explain why concerted efforts are *cumulative*. The conditions of work, incomes, and status of one work group, if accepted as

[13] In a recent study we concluded there was a real distinction between the wildcat strike, that is, the product of internal strength and the one which arises out of the internal weakness of a group. Leonard Sayles, "Wildcat Strike," *Harvard Business Review*, XXXII, No. 6, November-December, 1954, p. 47.

[14] Mason Haire and Josephine H. Gottsdanker, "Factors Influencing Industrial Morale," *Personnel*, XXVII, 1951, p. 453.

a reference base by another group, can provide an enduring challenge and target. For example, it is rare that a semiskilled group, no matter how "close" they are, will obtain working conditions comparable to those of a skilled trade, but they can keep trying.

In the same way, a threat to an important group benefit can galvanize its members to action. Rarely is the threat completely dissipated, and even if it is, the success experience may be all that is needed to teach the employees involved that concerted action is rewarding.

Power begets power—once this lesson is learned it is likely to be repeated. The prestige that groups gain both from the benefits they win, and from their success in winning them (insofar as status is often a prerequisite for self-confidence in plant bargaining), provides a further impetus for continued activity.

Another way of assessing these relationships is to look for a moment at dissatisfaction. We have really been saying that there are two kinds of grievances. On the one hand, we have the major long-run problems of relative plant status. Here a group is attempting to carve out a more permanent and satisfactory position for itself, in terms of relative earnings and working conditions. It may never achieve what it accepts as success, but the process of "carving out" in itself provides a feeling of success or failure. Superimposed on the pattern of major problems are the minor day-to-day irritations: an employee is disciplined harshly; a shortage of parts reduces incentive earnings; work is shifted to another department; and so on.[15] Some of these groups —the obsolescent ones—are attacking what are essentially insoluble problems; others have literally lifted themselves by their bootstraps and are for the present "at peace with the world"; some are in midstream in what could easily be a decade-long struggle to improve their job; and some have given up in defeat.

POWER, SATISFACTION, AND PRODUCTIVITY

It is a long step to move from observations of group behavior to questions of morale and productivity. These factors are much less tangible and less observable, but certainly no less important. We have already implied that the expressions of aggression on the part of some groups often do not involve any increase in satisfaction. The immediate target is but a "last straw" following a whole series of unresolved and often unexpressed grievances. But what about the highly

[15] I am indebted to David Riesman for suggesting in correspondence this concept of the grievance process.

legalistic groups that know what they want, and presumably know how to get it? We surmise that the groups having effective power do experience increased satisfaction. Management was likely to comment, in answer to our questions about these groups, that, although they had many grievances they were not necessarily poor workers. Similarly, turnover did not seem to be a problem here as it did in many of the less consistently active departments. Our third basis of appraisal, still an indirect one, was in terms of the leadership of these groups. Over and over management representatives described the informal leaders of these groups as "excellent workers," "slated for promotion," and "conscientious workmen." This was not often the case where the group's behavior had been Erratic or Apathetic. Their leaders were more likely to be unsatisfactory employees.

Although such evaluations are certainly subject to serious bias, it is significant that workers whose "troublemaking" and "unjustified grievances" were resented, could still be seen as productive and efficient. We would have expected quite the opposite result.

Dr. George Strauss in an unpublished study of two groups of insurance salesmen observes that high grievance activity and high productivity (in terms of sales of new policies) were positively correlated. Most striking was the fact that the high grievance group was also most vocal in criticizing management and supporting union penalties against strikebreakers and employees who appeared to be "too friendly" to the company during a period of hostile union-management relations. Nevertheless, they outproduced all of their more loyal colleagues.[16]

Our own conclusion is that in the long run, the worker's confidence in his ability to protect himself and to secure equitable treatment is essential to satisfactory morale and eventually to productivity itself. Many of the so-called legalistic groups undoubtedly enjoyed this high level of group confidence and group power. The same situation facilitated an efficient and systematic method of resolving conflicts; grievances did not fester. Viewed over a short period of time their perception of a need to pressure management or the union might result in production blockages. Over a longer period of time, however, they would tend to be above average in effort expended on management goals. Put in another way, successful *upward* initiations (through the formal and informal grievance procedure) releases productivity.

The same factors would contribute to a more healthy relationship with the union. Such groups would be likely to support and take

[16] Private communication.

some responsibility for the leadership of that organization. As we shall consider in a later section, this positive attitude can be of major significance to the entire plant's system of industrial relations.

Researchers in industrial relations have been overly impressed with the workers' need for *social* satisfactions on the job. Undoubtedly there is truth in Mayo's observations on the mule-spinning department of a textile plant: isolated workmen become obsessive and less productive, and these conditions improve when the opportunity for social interaction is provided.[17] It is significant however that Mayo later modified his original hypothesis to take into account the effect of the *change itself* on worker attitudes; that is, he recognized that management's willingness to make changes that improved working conditions was interpreted as a favorable sign by the workers and was in part responsible for their increased efforts.

Of equal importance in encouraging productivity may be the factor of *experiencing group solidarity and success in attaining economic satisfaction.* In a number of the studies of the Survey Research Center, "pride in work group" is one of the major correlates, and one of the few consistent correlates of high productivity.[18] It is not unreasonable to assume that groups develop such pride, in part, out of the experience of unity and success in pursuing common objectives. We have seen many instances of the reverse, where failure to develop satisfactory cohesion resulted in mutual recriminations. On the other hand, the *esprit de corps* of a group that has proven itself (to itself) in a difficult grievance case is noteworthy. There is real satisfaction in the experience of having maintained unity under trying circumstances to win a difficult objective.

THE TOTAL PLANT AS AN ENVIRONMENTAL FACTOR

Also to be taken into account in explaining the industrial relations climate of a plant is the total structure of that organization, not only that of the constituent departments or work units.

Plants which are primarily assembly or line operations or where crew activities predominate seemed to be very different in their climate of industrial relations from plants in which individual or batch operations were the dominant structure.

Again the difference was not a simple linear function. Interde-

[17] Elton Mayo, *The Human Problems of an Industrial Civilization,* Graduate School of Business Administration, Harvard University, Boston, Mass., 1933, pp. 41–52.

[18] Cf. Nancy C. Morse, *Satisfactions in the White-Collar Job,* Institute for Social Research, Ann Arbor, Mich., 1953, pp. 59–61.

pendent plants (assembly and crew operations), which lacked strong, individual operation work groups with some status, comprised the polar cases in the sample. Among them were numbered the very best—and the worst—industrial relations records. These plants seemed to have more than their share of union-management cooperation and/or complete absence of conflict, and also more than their share of situations where the union ran rampant, and where they were constantly threatened by irresponsible strike activity. The other plants with more individual operation departments were rarely as good or as bad in the matter of industrial relations; they clustered in the middle ranges. Most job shop-type plants, also lacking homogeneous concentrations of single jobs, were similar to assembly-line plants in occupying polar positions.

Our own explanation of this contrast is admittedly speculative and tentative. We propose this hypothesis: Where the plant lacks strong occupationally oriented work groups, the union leader tends to be more independent of the members' judgment and feelings. This independence can result in the development of highly cooperative relationships with management, relationships which might be doomed to failure in other situations where the prejudices and fears of specific rank and file groups (or their excessive demands) would cause the overthrow of any officer who was too much in the good graces of management. However, this can be a highly dangerous situation for management as well, for it may explain those instances where a small officer clique dominates the plant and irresponsibly creates ceaseless turmoil.

We suggest, furthermore, that where work groups are well organized internally they demand the constant attention of the union leadership. The latter must be able to respond to the grievances and feelings of such groups in a manner that may make real union-management cooperation difficult, if not impossible. The selfishness of the individual work groups may prevent concessions where each makes a sacrifice for the greater good of all. However, such groups are also excellent "watch dogs." The union leadership cannot steer an autonomous course, creating strife for purely personal or political objectives. These groups are too conscious of their economic needs to permit a situation to deteriorate, as some we have observed, so that management eventually abandoned the plant because of the impossibility of insuring continuous, economic production.

It should be noted that there is a distinction between local unions which must respond to the demands of several strongly united interest groups and locals completely dominated by a single interest group.

There were only one or two cases in our sample which appeared to be in the latter category. Unfortunately it was unclear as to what the longer run effects of such domination by a single group might be. Our impression, however, was that this was a somewhat unstable condition, although the union-management pattern was similar to the situation where no single group had that much power.

We are suggesting that open conflict situations often reflect the inability of the rank and file to make themselves heard. They lack the stable group strength that could permit them to control the union. The leadership then, not necessarily because of planned malevolence, but because of lack of membership checks, becomes a group apart. Where it is comprised of highly aggressive personalities the results can be continuous and destructive strife. When the membership is not able to control the leadership, the union may be running rampant without actually satisfying the basic dissatisfaction of the members. In fact the frustrations involved, particularly the loss of earnings due to strikes and slowdowns, may only aggravate the employees and serve as fertile ground for still more unsatisfying demonstrations.

We received information about at least one well publicized case of union-management cooperation where the union functioned as a highly autonomous unit. After a period, management became concerned with the long-run problems of having a union leadership that took so much initiative in turning down member grievances and jointly administering a new production standards program. Unlike most of the locals we had studied previously, which had learned through painful experience the value of shying away from joint responsibility for unpopular decisions, these leaders actively sought out new situations in which they could share the authority role with management.

While many managements might consider this a utopian situation, where the union takes such responsibility for imposing relatively unpleasant decisions on its membership, the company in question discovered that this paradise had its disadvantages. The union functioned less successfully as a communication channel to management; serious sources of discontent were not systematically being uncovered, and often the company had to take the initiative in ferreting out the sources of what were obviously serious problems which the union had squelched. In return for the union assuming management functions, the company recognized that they had to assume certain union responsibilities.

Fifteen years ago Dr. Eliot Chapple foresaw this problem with union-management cooperation when he wrote:

> There is . . . the case in which union officials and members of management achieve a good adjustment and an equilibrium as a result of a much higher frequency of interaction with each other than that which the union leaders have with their members. . . . These weaknesses, the result of the relations of union leaders to management, show the necessity of a careful definition of these relations so that the union *can operate as a compensatory mechanism* and thus reduce the disturbances in the factory and increase the morale of its members.[19] [Italics mine.]

Chapple also concludes that union officials in conflict situations, by increasing their initiations to members of the rank and file when they themselves are under pressure from management, become very much "like the first line supervisors in the company." [20] Thus a vicious circle is created in these plants where day-to-day problems do not work themselves out through the grievance process. The leaders, lacking strong group support and thus failing to get management to move, begin pressuring the rank and file for more activity. To the membership this just adds to the burden of downward pressures already coming from their supervisors, and the result is a more disturbed, lower morale group of employees. The grievance process fails to work in these types of plants as a compensatory mechanism.

All this would cause one to conclude that there is a delicate balance in the relation of union leaders to their members and to management. Only in certain well prescribed situations, such as some of those described above, will the presence of the union serve to improve overall employee morale and serve as a stabilizing force within the plant community.

New forms of technology, such as the methods associated with automation, may serve to break up established groups and fragment the social structure of the plant. In many plants the trend toward more continuous work-flow systems, increasing differentiation of work, and greater numbers of subgroupings of employees clearly foretells drastic shifts in the industrial relations of the organization.[21]

Profitability. Another total plant factor, the significance of which is somewhat difficult to evaluate, is the profitability variable. There is some evidence that in marginal operations management is more likely to turn to the union for help in improving productivity. They

[19] Eliot D. Chapple, "The Analysis of Industrial Morale," *The Journal of Industrial Hygiene and Toxicology*, 24, 1942, p. 169.

[20] *Ibid.*, p. 168.

[21] Cf. W. H. Scott, J. A. Banks, A. H. Halsey, and T. Lupton, *Technical Change and Industrial Relations*, Liverpool University Press, Liverpool, England, 1956, pp. 19–20.

may also be less resistant to individual or group demands for concessions under threats of slowdowns and stoppages. In critical situations, therefore, the power of some of these groups may be magnified by the economic distress of the firm. In the highly profitable, successful operation, management can afford to be more independent and resistant to such encroachments. In turn, this resistance reduces somewhat the influence of the stronger work groups.

We really need to know more about the "laws of combination" pertaining to these concerted interest groups. What is the difference in the effect of having *one* as compared to *several groups* with a reputation for high concerted activity in the plant? For example, we observed in plants with limited numbers of such groups, departments such as toolrooms, inspectors, and materials handlers, which otherwise might be overshadowed, become more highly active.

It is possible to distinguish among plants on the basis of the kind of group that is the most active in challenging management and the union. Thus in any given plant at a given time, the real hot spots or tension areas may be in one of two or three quite different kinds of groups. We have seen situations where the highly legalistic group which never tires of comparing its benefits with those of other groups in the plant is the focus for industrial relations problems. In other situations the less predictable, Erratic work teams are the source of periodic, if not continuous, plant turmoil. It is also conceivable that some groups we have categorized as Conservative would renew their aggressive activity after a quiescent period as a result of finding themselves in a relatively worse economic position because of the greater political efforts made by other groups. The conclusion, of course, is that these are by no means similar plants in terms of their industrial relations climate.

Further exploration of the relationship between the overall technology of the plant and the behavior of various work groups and the union should provide a fruitful field of additional research. At the moment at least, our observations certainly do not qualify as conclusions. They only suggest the potential value of future research.

Summary

In this chapter we have sought to clarify the underlying motivations for the kinds of protest actions characteristic of the four group patterns of behavior. In order to do this we emphasized the possibility of certain shifts over time, that is, the movement of a work group from one category to another. We also sought to explore the triggering mechanism for concerted actions. Considered were intergroup comparisons of relative advantages, threats from management and the past success or failure of the group in applying pressures.

We concluded that the important difference lay between the personal, spontaneous-interest groups (Apathetic and Erratic) and the premeditative, legalistic ones (Strategic and Conservative). We believe that the same dichotomy is observable in certain *total plant patterns of industrial relations activity*. The technology of certain plants can predispose the total worker-management relationships toward a high degree of cooperation or toward the opposite pole, that of hostility. These are the closely integrated plants, or job shop type plants. Other plants, due to the inherent strength of individual occupational groups, tread a middle ground. They have less potential for noteworthy cooperation, but also less inclination toward the open conflict type of situation.

The connecting link between work group behavior and total plant industrial relations experience is the leadership factor. We examined the quality of leadership preferred or selected by the four types of groups. Our conclusion was that the dominating, go-it-alone type of leader, who was expressing deep-seated aggressions in his challenge to management, arose most frequently in Apathetic and Erratic groups. Just as such union leaders were unwilling or unable to exercise restraints on their actions, we believe that the employees of certain structural types of plants are unable to exercise control over their union leadership. These also comprised our best examples of highly cordial union-management relationships and destructively hostile ones as well. While management never "had it so bad" (or so good) in organizations comprised of strong self-interest groups seeking to better their own positions, this kind of environment provided greater predictability and stability.

The next chapter concentrates on more specific implications of this kind of group behavior analysis for management and the union as organizations.

chapter 5

Implications for management and the union: administering groups

We have tried to learn more about the reactions of workers to their industrial environment when they are combined into interest groupings. In the process we have suggested that differences in their behavior may fall into some definite and predictable pattern related to several factors, primarily attributable to technology. These factors include the size and relative prestige of the group, the amount of worker control over the pacing of the work, the degree of homogeneity or similarity or interest within the group, and, most importantly, the relative independence or dependence of the employees in their work relationships—the patterning and flow of work within the organization.

There are a number of obvious implications for personnel management and the union organization flowing from the concept of work groups struggling for self-betterment.

In the belief that predictions about the behavior of different types of pressure groups can be made, we now consider the possible values of such predictions to companies and unions.

Foremost we suggest that successful execution of industrial relations policies on the part of both organizations requires some comprehension of the distribution of the power centers in the plant organization. The active representatives of management and the union experience the effects of this structure daily and are usually aware of certain differences between hot spots and "places where you can pretty much do whatever you want to." But they often do not relate this conception of the plant to the formulation of policy. Greater conscious awareness of the impact of these groups should improve industrial relations practice. The material which follows has this objective as its goal.

Implications for Management

MANAGEMENT ATTITUDES TOWARD INTEREST GROUPS

We have found a number of management policies based on fallacious reasoning:

(1) Some management officials insist they "never succumb to worker pressures." We visited no plants in which there was not obvious evidence that the degree of unity and strength of the group directly contributed to their ability to win certain concessions. The grievance procedure itself was nearly always a channel for bargaining as well as for redress.

(2) A large number of executives echoed the sentiments of this manager: "Working conditions and the quality of worker employed are the major determinants, if not the only determinants of the quality of your industrial relations." Yet we found numerous instances where departments with relatively poor working conditions (e.g., metal plating) were completely passive regarding better facilities and rates. On the other hand, many good areas constantly tried to become even better places to work.

(3) Similarly, the belief that getting rid of the few "troublemakers" who spoil things for everybody would convert a difficult department into a "well behaved" one was often doomed to failure. Somehow many of these trouble centers continued to attract troublemakers who would "stir up the men." When one was removed, another took his place.

(4) A surprising number of companies follow the policy of appointing what they call the "behind the scenes leader" to a management position, often in the same department. They too operate under the assumption that the leader shapes group attitudes, rather than what seems to be more valid reasoning: that the group selects as a leader the kind of person who reflects its own feelings. Management is often disappointed to find that the new supervisor has no greater control over the obstreperous group than did the man he

replaced. In fact, if he is considered a "turncoat," he may do more poorly because he has the additional problem of change of role to cope with.

What then are the positive recommendations that can be made?

SELECTION AND DEVELOPMENT OF SUPERVISION

To date emphasis has generally been placed on developing "qualities of good supervision," on the assumption that these are universally applicable. Although there are undoubtedly certain general principles that are applicable to almost any relationship where there are both superior and subordinate present, it is important to recognize that the behavior of the supervisor is only a part of the relationship. What is appropriate behavior for the supervisor is conditioned, to a substantial degree, by the reactions of his subordinates. The supervisor does not supervise in a vacuum. Each step he takes produces a covert or overt response on the part of those supervised and, as we have seen, the response will vary with the work group supervised.

Chinoy also suggests that the "type of work" being supervised has an important effect on the worker's evaluations of the supervisor. His example relates to our previous observations concerning the differences between industrial occupations with ambiguous standards and those with clearly defined output standards:

> While men recognized that a considerate and understanding foreman could turn up anywhere, even in final assembly, and that a nagging crotchety, authoritarian foreman might be found in the departments with the best jobs, there was a widespread feeling that off-production jobs were more likely to be blessed with good supervision than were those in production divisions . . . This feeling came not from any apparent superiority in the quality of foremen in off-production departments, but from differences in the character of work assignments and the resulting differences in the responsibilities of supervision. In production departments, foremen are chiefly concerned with seeing that workers maintain standards which are set on the basis of systematic job analysis . . . The supervisor of machine operators has a constant record of the value of output from each machine with which to appraise workers' efforts and efficiency. Failure to meet job standards will quickly invite criticism and possibly threats or sanctions from the foreman. But in off-production jobs, the foreman does not usually have such sharply defined standards against which to check performance. He assigns the work to be done, and as long as it is completed adequately in what seems to be a reasonable time, workers need not fear supervisory criticism.[1]

[1] Eli Chinoy, *Automobile Workers and the American Dream*, Random House, New York, 1955, p. 73.

Based on our own study we would not expect that a supervisor who is successful in dealing with the men in Department A would necessarily be just as successful in dealing with the men in Department B. Quite different skills and temperaments may be required, depending in part upon what Department A and Department B encompass in the way of pressure groups.

As we might expect, the largest turnover among supervisors, concentration of complaints about current supervision, and general concern over the problem of good supervision were in those departments and work groups which demonstrated Erratic and Strategic behavior patterns, where concerted activity was greatest. Management felt that these were the areas which required the "strongest leadership," the "most able" supervisors, men "who were not afraid to stand up and assert their authority," and "command recognition as leaders." These rather general attributes are not easy to define or assess in potential candidates.

However, this much is clear: the companies under observation assumed that such groups required the most skillful leaders, and that the more passive departments provided much less challenge to their foremen. Our own conclusions diverge from these simple maxims.

We would agree, for example, that the typical Erratic group requires the ablest type of supervisor. He should be a stable self-confident type of person. The likelihood that even the most intelligent decision-making and skilled leadership performance will be greeted by periodic demonstrations would discourage many men of lesser talents. Almost by definition, these groups do not respond in any completely predictable manner. This very lack of predictability, the possibility that abrupt failure is just around the corner, is difficult to tolerate. Where the supervisor is already personally insecure, it is likely that such experiences will be shattering to him. By either blaming himself and adopting the reactions of a man ridden with guilt, or by applying recriminations to his subordinates, he is likely to lose control of the situation. Aggressive reactions in the group to the personal frustrations involved will further aggravate the problems he faces.

The reaction of his superiors is also a critical factor. They must recognize that the group which he supervises is not rational in all its behavior, and that even the perfect supervisor could not expect to eliminate all concerted activity. Many of these activities are generic to the group itself and its position within the total plant organization. By sympathetic understanding of this problem and by supporting the supervisor in his difficult role, they may bolster his position and strengthen his self-confidence.

However, such support will only be successful in the long run when the man in direct charge of the group is highly stable and able to comprehend the group forces with which he is working. He must be able to observe that certain Erratic reactions may be beyond his control, at least as far as their initiation is concerned. His greatest strength can come in learning how to cope with the reactions in such a way that long-run problems are minimized.

Of almost equal difficulty from the point of view of supervision are those groups which show almost no concerted behavior, the Apathetic groups. There is little evidence of leadership within such a group, and the department often seems to be fractionalized into a number of competing or antagonistic cliques and subgroups. Under these circumstances the supervisor will have great difficulty in securing any consistent reaction from his subordinates. A given decision will be strongly supported by one group and almost equally strongly opposed by one or more others. Consequently, attempts to win agreement prior to acting (via consultative supervision) may be doomed to failure from the start. Almost by definition there is no consensus within the group. Morale is not overtly bad, and it is in this deception that the real danger lies. Because few protests or requests are made directly, the supervisor may be lulled into a sense of false security. Beneath the surface worker dissatisfaction may be rampant and may be affecting the work effort.

Thus, the supervisor must have a clear comprehension of the structure of the work group, plus ability in working with a complex set of forces. He also needs the rare skill of being able to balance the interests and demands of a number of cliques.

At first glance a group showing Strategic patterns of behavior may seem one of the most difficult to deal with because of its well-organized militancy. However, its predictability, its concentration of leadership in a small core group, and its forthright, outspoken nature provide a more receptive environment to effective leadership than do work groups demonstrating Apathetic and Erratic patterns. As long as the supervisor recognizes that the men in his particular department are going to be hypercritical, are going to challenge policies that are accepted without question in other departments, and are often going to be the pattern setters for the entire plant, he can develop the necessary "negotiating skills" that will maintain operations. He must also be temperamentally able to accept upward initiations of action from subordinates. If the group is unionized, the supervisor needs to be thoroughly familiar with collective bargaining and the structure and function of the local union. This means being up to the minute in comprehending not only the literal meaning of the union contract, but also its numerous applications to specific situations throughout the plant, many of which will represent informal agreements. Management may have to help him develop that unique ability: to be able to accept challenges to his authority in such a way that his subordinates are assured they will get a real hearing for their complaints, yet in the process retaining the leadership of his department.

Particularly difficult in the supervision of such groups are issues concerned with output standards. If personal judgment factors predominate and standards cannot be precisely controlled, the supervisor will have to rely more on his own skills to get group acceptance of reasonable productivity. He will not be able to rely on the fiat of the standards department as do supervisors in many machine-paced groups.

Supervisors of a Strategically oriented group will be able to utilize its informal leaders to facilitate the supervisory job. Because of the essential unity that prevails, the informal leader accurately reflects the sentiments of the group and, in turn, has some influence on group opinions. Thus the supervisor can sound out group sentiment by consulting with the leader before committing himself to what could be an irrevocable decision. Similarly he can often gain the support of the leader for changes in the department by incorporating some of the leader's suggestions concerning ways of making the innovations more palatable and acceptable to employees. The leader then assists the supervisor in getting acceptance by virtue of his own prestige and his ability to communicate with all the factions in the group. To repeat, this approach is not universally applicable. Group cohesiveness, which insures some unity in the leadership function, and group confidence in its position in the plant, which insures the selection of relatively stable individuals as leaders (not highly aggressive personalities), are essential prerequisites to this method of supervision.

A number of the managers we interviewed reported satisfaction with the supervisors of Conservative groups. These supervisors, however, may have been receiving somewhat more credit than they deserved. Conservative groups respond more readily to what have come to be accepted practices of "good supervision." They can take responsibility, they are cohesive and can speak affirmatively, and when they have complaints, these usually reflect objectionable conditions.

Often Conservative leaders make able supervisors, and even more important, the groups readily accept such a change in an employee's role. These employees are accustomed to respecting their most skilled and able colleagues and are able to transfer this respect to the man's new position as supervisor. In many cases the management's choice for promotion is an obvious one from the point of view of the group. The transition is thus a painless one, as compared to the serious role conflicts often confronting the newly promoted supervisor in departments where potential leadership skill is not evident to management and employees alike.

Another way of saying this is that job skill is usually positively correlated with informal group status for work areas we have called Conservative.

Personality Requirements. In general we have found that work groups differ in the quality of supervision they prefer. In a sense, one can envision a range of supervisory types in *demand*, just as there are differences in the type *supplied* by various supervisors. Although supervisors can acquire specific leadership skills and social sensitivities, the total relation they establish with their subordinates is to a great extent conditioned by their unique personalities.

It would appear that groups in which the workers are technically interdependent tend to establish strong personal affiliations with their supervisors. The successful supervisors in such groups identified in every way with their men, saw themselves as defenders of their subordinates, and were often emotionally committed to a long-run relationship with the department. This affiliation affected not only their relations with their own department, but also with fellow supervisors and higher management. Being so closely attached to their workers, they were often in conflict with top management over its treatment and recognition of the group. They were often reluctant to mingle with other supervisors at the same level as themselves. Such men may disqualify themselves for promotion although they are highly effective in their present positions. (Management, however, still retains the problems of justifying their being passed over in the promotional process and providing them with other job satisfactions.)

In his own way, this type of supervisor is conscientious in looking out for the interests of his company. He often sees his men as giving more to the company than their share, not less, as others may believe. If their bosses in turn accept the fact that expressions of loyalty, just like patterns of supervision, will differ among individuals and departments, they can adjust to such a supervisor's behavior. This kind of relation cannot be entered into by all supervisors, nor should it be, for under many circumstances a man who thrives on this type of personalizing his role will be well on his way to failure in living up to the demands of his job.

In less skilled departments such supervisors present problems to the union. Union leaders report they have difficulty handling the problems of "prima donna" groups whose supervisor has helped convince them that they are more important than any other department in the plant. As a result of this inflated sense of their own importance, their grievance demands become unreasonable.

In addition, we have noted that persons engaged in interdependent operations, particularly those that have experienced an internal apprenticeship system, capped by a crew chief, are frequently more tolerant of relatively autocratic leadership than are work groups that have never experienced this kind of initiation process. Very serious transition problems can arise when a supervisor who has demonstrated a high degree of identification with, and support for, one of these groups is replaced. Rarely can the new man become the equal of his predecessor in the eyes of the group, and for that matter, the work group is unlikely to give him the chance to prove his stature and allegiance.

EVALUATING SUPERVISORY PERFORMANCE

One other distinction may be of significance. As others have observed, there is a tendency for supervisors of interdependent operations to relate themselves to the total group as a group rather than to the members as individuals.[2]

Where there is a crew chief responsible for the activities of the men in the crew, the natural tendency is for the supervisor to "negotiate" with him as the representative or informal leader of the group. On the other hand, in batch production, the supervisor tends to relate himself to the employees as individuals.

In both cases the supervisor may be neglecting the responsibilities of his position. As we have seen in the case of the hammershop, the position of the crew chief is an ambiguous one. His point of view and interests may be contrary to some of those of his men. While recognizing his superior skill and status, they may resent his advantages and the control he wields. Thus, accepting the ideas of the crew chief as representative of all the men in the crew may be misleading as to their real sentiments and likely future behavior.

Yet the neglect of the informal leader's position in the group in the

[2] A. K. Rice and E. L. Trist, "Institutional Determinants of Changes in Labour Turnover," *Human Relations,* V, 1952, pp. 361–362.

case of individual operation departments is equally shortsighted. Again, as we have noted in earlier sections, where the group is tightly knit, it is efficient as well as strategic to utilize its leadership as representative of the group, rather than to deal with a collection of individuals. This procedure saves energy and often permits more realistic adjustment of potential conflict situations before they become serious.

These possibilities suggest that attitude studies which attempt to measure the supervisor's effectiveness may be subject to some bias. Some of these studies attempt to measure the extent to which the supervisor consults with his subordinates. However, the degree of power residing in the group itself may condition the response. Members of groups that feel themselves incapable of seriously questioning any management decision may see their supervisor as an autocrat, while the same foreman, if he were heading up a strong, active department, might be characterized by those workers as democratic and willing to let them participate in the formulation of solutions to department problems.

In the same vein, management training programs, as well as assessments of their effectiveness, can stray from reality when they neglect the *kind of group* which the supervisor leads. Universal platitudes may be far less effective in providing the tools for effective supervision than realistic analyses of the distribution of effective power within the plant. To be sure, the supervisor needs to be given the "tools" to supervise, but one of the most important tools is the ability to analyze the characteristic behavior of his own subordinate group. Thus "canned" training programs that ignore the realities of the given plant and given department may be worse than useless; they may be dangerously misleading. This fact could explain, at least in part, the failure of some serious attempts to measure the results of supervisor training to show changes in employee attitudes and productivity.[3]

We are really saying that there are at least two variables to take into account in assessing supervision: the qualities of the supervisor and the qualities of the group. Too often the assumption is made that worker attitudes and morale are almost exclusively the product of external (to the group) factors, such as the qualities of the supervisor, intrinsic satisfaction provided by the work, and job security and income. This assumption ignores the real influence of the work group as an active agent in the process of shaping employee perceptions.

[3] E. A. Fleischmann, E. F. Harris, and W. E. Burtt, *Leadership and Supervision in Industry: An Evaluation of a Supervisory Training Program,* The Ohio State University, Columbus, Ohio, 1955.

FACTORS IN ASSESSING PLANT POWER STRUCTURE

To assist the supervisor in evaluating the type or types of groups with which he must deal and to make more realistic the provision of on-the-job training for first line administrators and the evaluations of their effectiveness, managers need to give more attention to internal assessments of their own organizations. In turn this will facilitate more intelligent placement of supervisors. While much attention has been given to the problem of matching employees to jobs at non-supervisory levels, almost no attention has been devoted to what may well be a more significant and fruitful area of study: the matching of personality characteristics of present and potential supervisors with the "demand" characteristics of the supervisor's job.

As we have reasoned, all first-line supervisors, even within similar manufacturing companies, do not have similar jobs; particularly, the demands which the subordinate group makes upon the supervisor vary enormously. It would be unreasonable to expect that the spans of control for different supervisors be identical. For Strategic and Conservative groups, for example, it could be much greater, we would assume, than for the others. The number of necessary contacts, supervisor to subordinate, should be less for these cohesive, predictable groups. All these considerations point to the need for greater sensitivity to the group structure of the plant.

The following appear to be useful points of departure for such an analysis:

(1) *The Benefit Structure.* On occasion it may be worthwhile for management to take a long run look at changes that have taken place in the distribution of benefits in the plant. To assess the impact of the specific interest groupings in a given plant, management should try to measure the following:

A. Is there any pattern in the distribution of the re-evaluation of jobs? Have certain groups tended to have more jobs reclassified upward than others?

B. If incentives are utilized, have there been any changes in the relative total earnings among jobs in the plant over the past five or ten years? Is there any concentration of "loosened" rates in particular departments? In one sense, the existence of an incentive payment system or piecework system is also an incentive for just the kind of group actions to which this study refers. Such systems of income distribution provide that additional element of flexibility which encourages pressures designed to improve the worker's relative position.[4]

C. Taking into account total earnings (base rates, incentive, and overtime payments), has there been a trend toward converging or diverging earnings among departments? We believe that in some plants, quite apart from any formal union policy, the absence of strong groups brings about a *convergence* in the earnings of various groups. In some of these plants it was expected that men on lower-rated jobs would work harder under their incentive plan in order to end up with about the same take-home pay as men on higher-rated jobs. On the other hand, in other plants there was a rapid *divergence* in earnings between groups, when strong groups were effective in getting their claims to higher rates and looser standards recognized.

The answers to such questions as these should provide some clues as to the effect of concerted interest behavior in the plant.

(2) *Internal Union Politics.* Management also needs to take a closer look at the internal life of the union. To some this has been a forbidden area since the Wagner Act first forbade interference with unions and their representatives chosen by employees. However, management needs to know the extent to which the union leadership represents the real power distribution in the plant. One management representative with experience in a number of different companies drew these conclusions:

> . . . In many plants I've seen there are one or two "rump groups" that pretty much get what they want. They are ready to ignore the grievance procedure if they think they can get more without it. Sometimes these powerful groups are not represented on the bargaining committee of the union. This just complicates negotiations because the elected leaders can never give you a firm answer. From our point of view we would rather have such groups represented in the leadership; it would save a great deal of checking back and, we feel, would improve management-union relations.

If there are serious defections from the union, and the chance of dual unionism, management needs to be informed because such situations are likely to bring with them serious conflict. Although the company cannot interfere with the results of union elections, an awareness of which groups are likely to be dissatisfied, because they are not directly represented, may facilitate improved handling of their grievances. The company can be alert to the political realities: the union has to respond to those groups which are most vocal in relating

[4] Cf. Robert R. Roy, "Do Wage Incentives Reduce Costs?" *Industrial and Labor Relations Review,* V, 1952, pp. 195–208.

themselves to the leadership. As a result, "weak" groups may need additional attention paid them and increased sensitivity to their needs.

(3) *The Meaning of Union Agreements.* In a realistic sense, management will always be in the position of having to make changes in the organization of work, in job standards, and in working conditions that will meet resistance. That is, given the best leadership techniques available, there will be occasions when unpopular changes must be introduced. The question then arises, what kind of opposition can management expect? How accurately can they predict the nature and extent of the resistance of the employee group affected?

Even when there is a union in the picture, their best assessment of employee attitudes often will not be adequate. For example, we have observed instances where the union leadership—even those local leaders who presumably were close to the situation—agreed in good faith to certain changes in job classifications or performance standards. The managers put the agreements into effect only to discover they had a revolt on their hands. These completely unexpected refusals to accept any changes then forced management to take unplanned-for drastic action to achieve the necessary conformity.

We are not suggesting that the ability to predict resistance areas always will enable management or the union to devise successful means of coping with the situation before trouble occurs. However, knowing what to expect does help insure that neither the managers nor the union leaders find themselves having to save face vis-à-vis their employees or their members. Important areas of maneuver can be lost by public commitments which have been premised on faulty knowledge.

Therefore, we need to develop in-plant intelligence service; but this step is not primarily a problem of better communications, or the identification of good informers. It is often easy to learn about existing worker sentiments. What has been lacking until now, however, has been adequate emphasis on the potential *results* of these sentiments in terms of actual behavior. Feelings of inequity in one group may result in a mild protest followed by a resumption of good working relations, and relatively similar feelings in another group can signal a potential violent eruption. These are the cases where two and three month slowdowns or strikes follow union-management *agreements!*

Thus a periodic review of the kinds of internal pressures to which management and the union are subject, as well as the effects of these pressures, both actual and potential, may enable an organization to conduct its personnel program on the basis of a realistic appraisal of internal plant conditions. Although such variables may enormously complicate the job of the administrator, ignoring them does not minimize their effect.

CRITERIA FOR THE IDEAL WORK GROUP

Another way of assessing the significance of these work groups is to attempt to list the criteria of desirable interest group behavior, from management's point of view, in the areas we have been considering.

Portraying the "ideal" work group may not help the present-day administrator in converting his less-than-ideal ones. However, if attempts to relate technology to work group behavior prove valid, it may someday be possible to prescribe such types to the industrial engineer concerned with methods and layout. In the meantime the following criteria may be useful as bench marks in measuring work group performance in the plant community.

1. *Predictability and Consistency of Behavior.* The effective supervision of a work group requires that the supervisor be able to assess the attitudes and expectations of his subordinates. Much as this practice is often taken for granted, we have found work groups where such an assessment was almost impossible. Internal splits, lack of informal leadership, and real self-deception on the part of the rank and file make the supervisor's job a most difficult one.

> In one department of a large steel plant, the men threatened to strike unless they were granted overtime hours comparable to those enjoyed by most of the other departments in the plant at that time. Management was reluctant to change the work schedule, but finally agreed to add a sixth day of work. The supervisor and the union steward jointly canvassed the department to work out individual schedules, as the day off would have to vary for different workers. Upon completion of this arduous task the department voted down any change in hours, nullifying weeks of union pressure and their own chances of receiving premium pay. They could not agree on who should have week ends free.

Here was a case where the men could not express what they wanted, even when given the opportunity. It was likely at one point that they were going to strike for an objective they would not accept when it was attained!

We do not believe this is an exceptional case. There are many such work groups whose erratic behavior cannot be predicted, and therefore the supervision of such departments becomes most difficult.

These departments contrast sharply with the groups that are able to express clearly and consistently what they want. Although a manager may not always be able to accede to the requests of such a group, he can at least make plans to deal intelligently with a clearly defined situation.

2. *Representative Leadership Reflecting a Consensus in the Group.* We suggest that the supervisor's job is facilitated by the existence of a rank-and-file leader, whether formally elected as steward or informally accepted as spokesman. It becomes possible to consult with this individual rather than undertake the more time-consuming (and often less enlightening) task of interviewing each employee when the attitudes of the workers are the matter in question. Similarly, the leader often provides a communication link back to the employees for the interpretation and clarification of company policy. Work groups which are internally divided, where no single individual or small group can speak for the whole, are much more difficult to administer.

A qualification should be added to the preceding statements. The existence of a leader who can echo the sentiments of the group should not be confused with the source of worker attitudes. Such representatives are not necessarily opinion formers; they are usually merely spokesmen. Only work groups that are united and able to evolve a consistent pattern of ideas are likely to have such spokesmen.

3. *Responsibility for Controlling Union Activity.* In an earlier section we observed that serious problems may occur when the union leadership is not placed in the position of having to respond continuously to special interest groups. Such demands provide a healthy and appropriate focus for union activities within the plant, and union leaders themselves typically prefer rank-and-file groups that can take some initiative in framing specific demands. Management should prefer interest groups that take an active part in the union's internal life. As we have also noted, it is much easier to negotiate with a leadership that represents the real power structure of the plant. Rump groups, potential secessionists, and Apathetic departments only serve to complicate what is already a complicated process —collective bargaining.

4. *Security for Members during Periods of Change.* We believe that employees are more secure and more satisfied when they are members of groups that are effective in expressing and defending

rank-and-file points of view. Turnover, it is believed, will be greater when employees feel they are in a weak group, at the mercy of changes in supervision, management policies, and technology.

From the same point of view, it would seem that groups with self-confidence in their ability to prosecute justifiable grievances successfully would also not be fearful of increasing output. Restriction of output is basically a product of fear, fear that rates will be changed adversely, that too much will be demanded, that the very fast will be advanced or rewarded ahead of the slow, or that someone will lose his job. Such fears are of less significance when there are assurances, based on past experience, that group consensus is effective in winning justifiable grievances. These grievances often do not move through the procedure on their merits alone. Further, the ability to initiate favorable changes successfully to both management and union hierarchies is likely to have a favorable effect on group productivity. There is good evidence, as we have discussed, that the ability to compensate for all the day-to-day downward pressures by upward originations serves to release productivity. Therefore, where the work group is active in providing its members with mutual support, productivity should not be a problem.

The same factors hold for adjustment to new conditions. Technological change, new supervision, and new policies are feared most by groups which have little confidence in their ability to have some influence on the results of these changes. Management needs groups that can adjust to change, for change itself is the constant in most contemporary industrial organizations in the United States.

5. *Teamwork and Cohesiveness.* Particularly where there is interdependence among employees in the production process, management requires the coordination of the efforts of the members. However, such groups may be prone to internal differences, at least on the intercrew level or in the relations of crew chief to crew members. These are delicate areas and, where relations are good, the situation is a tribute to the leadership qualities of the crew chief and the supervisor.

It is also important for the informal group to include operations that are highly interdependent. We noted instances where management, in designing the formal organization and laying out the work flow, separated groups that should have been united (e.g., blind spots between groups that must coordinate).

There are also instances where the self-interest activity of small cliques divides workers who need to work together. For example, in one plant one of the major starting operations utilized two basic types of machines that were almost identical except for size. The larger machines utilized a three-man crew and the smaller required only one operator. In order to obtain certain seniority advantages (additional protection in the case of a work force reduction), the small machine operators lobbied for and won a separate seniority designation. As a result, operators are no longer transferable between these two pieces of equipment. Management now has a serious training problem because operators cannot be shifted. This situation has reduced the overall flexibility in the department and has made adjustments to changed work loads more difficult.

Thus teamwork is a function of the formal organization, the informal organization, and the skills of leadership that are employed.

6. *Balance between Reception and Resistance to Outside Stimuli.* A work group requires a certain degree of resistance to outside stimuli. There will be many temptations to follow some other group in demonstrating against unsettled grievances. However, a pattern of such contagious behavior indicates that the group lacks adequate independence. Further contagious actions are unlikely to clear the air. Rather, they build up frustrations because the final settlement with management rarely solves all the problems at issue, and each strike usually involves sacrifices for other groups. Such contagious strikes often take place in interdependent work areas, where the actions of one group cause many others to lose earnings.

Similarly, a group needs to be able to resist following the leadership of newcomers who have selfish interests or special grievances. The real troublemaker (not the appointed leader of the antagonistic group) can only flourish where the group lacks security and cohesiveness. While full and immediate acceptance of the ideas of outsiders or newcomers is a danger, so is the closed group which cannot tolerate the new colleague. Many crews, because of the close working relationships required, have been guilty of exclusiveness and prejudice that makes transfer and promotion of ethnic minorities a serious problem.

Somewhere between these two extremes—ready acceptance of all new people and ideas, and complete exclusiveness—is the desired optimum.

7. *A Trend toward Equilibrium.* We believe that in some industrial plants the concerted interest activities of the work groups are increasingly unstabilizing. That is, rather than leading toward a point of

equilibrium, the resultant of their pressure tactics is continued or increased pressure on the part of interest groups.

By equilibrium we mean a balance between the effective power of the groups and its position on a relative scale of plant benefits, so that there is no incentive for further pressuring activities. When this balance is absent the activities of one group trigger another group and eventually the first group is again motivated to "do battle." The spirals of the cycle may become increasingly broad as succeeding explosions are the result of more serious frustrations. There is then no tendency toward equilibrium.

On the other hand, we can envision a situation where groups gradually bring their scale of benefits in line with the resultant of rank-and-file attitudes and management beliefs. Until disturbed by some technological change, this distribution would be acceptable as parity, and self-interest activity would be minimal in the plant.

Of all our criteria, this is perhaps the most critical for harmonious industrial relations and long-run organizational growth.

Implications for the Union

ITS POLITICAL LIFE

We are beginning to comprehend that the unique contribution of American unionism is the shop level grievance procedure. In other countries trade unions have tended to concentrate either on the political front or on industry-wide or nation-wide collective bargaining. As we observed in another context, one of the most important factors in explaining the kinds and numbers of grievances entering this process is the strength and determination of the work groups involved.[5] In one sense the groups we have been talking about resemble the purely selfish economic men of classical theory. As Clark and others have pointed out, the concept of the union itself as mainly or exclusively a wage or employment maximizing institution departs radically from reality:

> It appears that one falls far short of understanding unions if one approaches them via the assumption that each is an economic bargaining unit, with a quantitatively defined objective which it pursues single-

[5] Leonard Sayles and George Strauss, *The Local Union*, Harper & Brothers, New York, 1953, pp. 59–69.

mindedly and undertakes to maximize, after the fashion familiar in the models of economic theory.[6]

The union is a political institution with all the attendant problems of survival and growth, prestige, and authority. But these interest groups such as we have described, based on occupation and proximity and whose members have almost complete identity of interest, approximate in their goals the single-minded objectives of the much maligned "economic man." In fact, we might argue that such an aggregation of individuals with similar objectives comes closer to the model of economic theory than any single individual could. The intricacies of personality, and the conflicting and ambiguous goals of security and mobility, prestige and anonymity that are interwoven in the warp and woof of the unique individual preclude a sustained drive toward the maximization of utility. Similarly, the institution of the union, like that of the corporation, is too complex in its structure and objectives to be so treated. Pure competition among units thrives within a highly specific environment of relatively small, undifferentiated participants to the market process. Although even our groups fall short of this criterion, their foundation in the purely *economic needs* of the employee bring them close to the ideal.

We have observed that those groups where identity of interest is most complete are the most vociferous in their demands. The sociological concept of status enters as an additional contributant to power. We can only hypothesize that prestige and group cohesion are highly correlated. We have also described some of the more obvious debilitating characteristics of these vested interest groups, such as workflow interdependence. And, finally, we have suggested that the total plant may be characterized on the basis of the kinds of interest group structures which it includes. It is hoped that these very tentative findings will contribute some impetus to further studies of this little touched branch of micro-economics, the internal labor market. This encompasses the interaction of individuals and groups within the framework of the industrial relations system of the plant, with its formal array of job classification, incentive, seniority, and promotional systems, as well as the less tangible benefit programs incorporated in the distribution of leniency, kinds of work, overtime hours, work standards, and all the rest. The growth of pension programs, tight seniority rules, and even guaranteed wages reduces sharply mobility outside of the plant structure. Within the confines

[6] J. M. Clark, "America's Changing Capitalism," in *Freedom and Control in Modern Society*, edited by M. Berger, T. Abel and C. Page, D. Van Nostrand, Co., New York, 1954, p. 201.

of the bargaining unit, however, the opportunities for movement even without changing jobs are manifold! Where some semblance of economic motivation is retained, our findings indicate they will be *magnified* in the context of the interest group.

Significantly, from the point of view of these groups, the entire internal political machinery of the local union is part of the grievance procedure. Through meeting attendance, petitions, and ballots, as well as by the spoken and written grievance, they make their wishes known.[7]

BETWEEN THE UNION AND ITS MEMBERSHIP

The union itself, at least at the local level, is shaped by the self-interest aggregations described above. This means, as we have noted, that the *absence* of strong interest groups as well as their presence has its impact. Persons who are politically active in local union affairs, we believe, are more autonomous where rank-and-file strength is lacking. The reverse situation introduces checks or controls upon the leaders. Lipset states this well:

> It may be stated as a general hypothesis that the greater the number of independent sources of power and status in an organization, the greater the possibility that alternative factions or parties will be established and oppose the incumbent party.[8]

He concludes, "One would therefore expect to find among unions in which the conditions for maintenance of oligarchy are not stable, a greater proportion of the two extremes, democratic institutions and dictatorial mechanisms." [9]

This idea lends support to the belief that unions, faced with a rank and file that is anxious and able to participate, will seek to build barriers against rank-and-file interference. The result is the unique situation where both the autocracy, stimulated by the fear of too much member power, and the democracy this member power represents exist side by side.

J. M. Clark is less optimistic about these same results attributable to pressure groups in terms of union democracy. Applying his analysis

[7] Leonard Sayles and George Strauss, "Some Problems of Communication in the Local Union," *Proceedings of the Fifth Annual Meeting of the Industrial Relations Research Association,* edited by L. Reed Tripp, Industrial Relations Research Association, Madison, Wis., 1953, pp. 144–149.

[8] Seymour Lipset, "The Political Process in Trade Unions! A Theoretical Statement," in Berger et al., *op. cit.,* p. 106.

[9] *Ibid.,* p. 117.

to unions we would expect that over the long run such unions would become less democratic.

> Political scientists hardly need to be told that, as government becomes more frankly a vehicle through which groups may directly promote their particular economic interests, the strains on the political and administrative machinery are enormously increased, and the democratic character of government seriously compromised.[10]

This type of problem is well illustrated by the experience of the UAW-CIO with their special councils. These councils, in a sense, are a compromise between craft and industrial unionism. Some of them have an industry base. For example, there is a truck and trailer council and a gear and axle council, each attempting to represent the special interests of workers employed by companies in their respective industries.

There is also a tool and die council and a die caster council.[11] They represent the special occupational interests of workers within particular branches of an industry.

Each of these councils is designed to make recommendations to the union negotiating committees in the various companies in which they are represented. Their function is to seek advantageous bargaining decisions, not just to exchange information concerning common problems. They provide tangible evidence of the strength and determination of particular occupational groups.

Recently the automatic screw machine operators attempted to form a similar council within the UAW on the presumption that they could make greater gains in their respective firms with some cross-company, formal bargaining organization of their own. The international officers, rather firmly, turned down the request for this new council and chastised some of the individuals involved in the incipient organization. Undoubtedly the problems of negotiation, as well as the problems of maintaining equilibrium in internal politics, are complicated by the existence of organized pressure groups.

The editors of *Fortune* are also pessimistic about the long-run effect of increasing recognition by the union member that he can promote his special interests at the expense of other work groups less able to wage an offensive:

[10] J. M. Clark, *op. cit.*, p. 204.

[11] These same groups have often been involved in attempts to form separate local unions at various locations. More recently there has been a complete re-evaluation of the position of skilled workers in the UAW, and they have received still greater autonomy.

> There is a price for these achievements of democratic unionism. The less class war, the more group greed: A quiet division of loot or assumption of privilege at the expense of less organized members of society. . . . The workers respond to this supposed sacrifice of vertical mobility by claiming more security. . . . The value of the union card is highest in a small unit: there is one local per company, if not per plant or even per department. . . . After a few years of service a man has amassed too big a stake to be willing to leave, even for a better job. They may also tend to convert the job into property and the work group into a closed guild. . . .[12]

We need to concern ourselves with this long-run picture of interest groups gaining increasing ascendancy within the structure of unions. We are left with the question whether the advantageous checks on individual union leaders are outweighed by danger stemming from the possibility that the stronger groups will take advantage of the weaker.

In our study of seniority problems we observed many cases where a strongly organized work group won privileges at the expense of weaker groups which had more legitimate claims.[13] As we concluded in that research, the introduction of bilaterally determined seniority privileges provides a major incentive for work groups to make aggressive excursions into the job-right territories of poorly defended fellow union members.

> Although this is certainly not always the case, the greatest success often goes to those workers who are able to support their grievances with the most political and economic power.[14]

THE GROUP'S EFFECT ON UNION MILITANCY

To this point we have considered the impact of interest group formation on one aspect of the union's internal life, the democratic-autocratic balance. It would be interesting to know whether such groups affect the degree of *militancy* or *conservatism* in their locals.

Kerr and Siegel believe that unions with a high propensity to strike are those with active memberships and a tendency toward factionalism.[15] However, we still are not sure that high participation in

[12] "The United States Labor Movement," *Fortune*, XLIII, February 1951, pp. 161–162.

[13] Leonard Sayles, "Seniority: An Internal Union Problem," *Harvard Business Review*, XXX, 1952, pp. 55–61.

[14] Sayles and Strauss, "Some Problems of Communication in the Local Union," *op. cit.*, p. 148.

[15] Clark Kerr and Abraham Siegel, "The Inter-Industry Propensity to Strike—an International Comparison," in *Industrial Conflict*, edited by A. Kornhouser, R. Dubin, and A. Ross, McGraw-Hill Book Co., New York, 1954, p. 198.

internal union political activity, which they believe is correlated with militancy, is also associated with occupational groupings. Kerr and Siegel find activity associated with "isolation" in society, for example, the miner or longshoreman.[16]

In both these situations strong identification with a segment of society rather than with specific "intervening groups," such as the occupational aggregations we have been discussing, helps explain the mass movement character of their relation to management and the union. These are the relationships at the extreme militancy pole of our continuum. We would expect to find other situations in which there is an absence of intervening groups, but where the work and community environment are more favorable to industrial peace. Here we would expect to find a significant absence of militancy and strikes. In the Kerr and Siegel study referred to above, agriculture, trade, and service industries in general fit this description.

It is very difficult to find evidence that political factions within the union are composed solely or primarily of special interests groups as we have described them. Factionalism appears to be much more a matter of personal and social differences than of economic ones. However, there are instances of a specific group, feeling that they have gotten far behind, seeking and obtaining union leadership.

The forces that affect the political make-up and policies of the union, just as those that affect our government, are much more complex than the kinds of pressure interests we have been describing. There is no simple explanation of the results of union elections or the policies of union leaders. Personality variables, religious and social prejudices, class background, and a whole complex of opportunistic political maneuvers combine with economic motivations in shaping the internal life of the local.

PARTICIPATION IN THE GRIEVANCE PROCEDURE

The operation of the grievance procedure as distinct from the internal life of the union is directly responsive to the kinds of pressures we have been discussing. Here group factors are more obviously of significance. Union leaders tend to draw a rather narrow line between "good" and "bad" groups in terms of their behavior in expressing and prosecuting their grievances. The following are composite descriptions provided by union leaders:

[16] *Ibid.*, pp. 191–193.

A. Weak Groups. These groups present serious problems for the leadership. They appear to specialize in petty problems which they expect the union leadership to solve successfully even though the grievance may have no basis in terms of the contract. They do little for themselves to settle problems, relying entirely on the union hierarchy. When a really important case comes along (where a significant precedent may be involved), the group may, with union prodding, demonstrate a spurt of activity which helps to convince management that the men are serious and determined. But before the case has been won, this interest disappears and the union has lost its support. This usually means that it has also lost an important precedent-setting case.

B. Prima Donnas. These are the groups that think they are more important than other people in the plant. Their inflated opinion of their relative worth is the cause of many embarrassing incidents. They may strike suddenly over an issue which the union cannot support, and their strength often serves to place union leadership in a most difficult position. Often the leaders are uncertain whether to support them, support the contract, or use common sense. Their frequent irresponsibility makes it difficult for the union to win other, more deserving cases.

C. The Mature Bargaining Groups. These groups have very few grievances that they cannot handle alone. Most of their problems are settled with supervision right on the floor by the men themselves. Their case will be a good one, which they support "right down to the wire." The men are patient and conduct themselves so that management recognizes their feelings about the importance of the issue.

The union's evaluation of these groups do not differ markedly from management's. Strong, consistent groups which have attained an equilibrium position are preferred over the internally unstable and disunited and the overly aggressive groups that have no sense of responsibility to the plant or union as a whole.

THE ORGANIZATIONAL STAGE

Of course, in organizing and establishing a local union, the international organization will feel the impact of the internal structure of the plant. Where strong groups are lacking, so may strong leaders be absent and attempts at organization may fail. In the early contact stage, the union may even have difficulty in securing men who can speak for any sizable proportion of the plant; and informants who can assess worker attitudes may be lacking. These "disorganized" situations present the same problems to the researcher who is seeking "opinion leaders." Such men do not exist in some kinds of industrial structures. The situation contrasts sharply with plants in which several to a half dozen key groups control things or at least have a degree of unity and purpose which enables them to work effectively in marshaling support for their objectives.[17] Here the incipient union organization can flourish.

Thus, for both management and the union, the attitudes and activities of these work groups (nestled between the individual employee-union member and the larger institutions of which they are a part) have substantial repercussions. Both management and union need to calculate their influence and power before attempting to put into effect any one of a broad range of policy decisions. Although these groups may not fit neatly into the organizational chart of either larger body (and as we shall see in the next chapter, they are not part of what we traditionally conceive as the informal organization), they are worthy of the administrator's constant attention.

Of course, they would be much less important if collective bargaining functioned like the textbook model: bargaining over the contract and grievances argued rationally in terms of that contract. The formal and the informal grievance process involves just as much bargaining as the negotiation of the labor agreement. In fact, in actual quantity of both issues and time, the day-to-day procedure probably involves substantially more. It is because of the importance of this type of bargaining that interest groups have such a crucial role in the plant community.

[17] Cf. the excellent study of the organizational process in a public utility by Dr. George Strauss, "Factors in the Unionization of a Utility Company," *Human Organization*, XII, 1953, pp. 17–25.

chapter 6

Research and theory on groups in industry

It is now in order to ask whether the patterns of work behavior and their motivations described in this study are consistent with existing theories and research on work groups in industry. Much research has been done in the field and we should relate the concepts derived from this project to the more inclusive framework provided by other studies.[1]

Much of this chapter, therefore, will be a review of other studies and a comparison of their findings with those described here. An important proportion of these other studies deals with the subject of informal organization (as distinct from formal organization) and this shall be our focus.

In the preceding chapters, for example, we have used such terms as work group, occupational group and interest group somewhat interchangeably. The concept of the *informal group* has been an important one in the field of industrial relations since the famous Western Electric researchers established their significance as "modifiers" of the behavior visualized by the planners of the formal organization.[2]

The most immediate and meaningful experiences of work for the individual are obtained in the context of his work group and his work

[1] This chapter, when in draft form, was the basis for the author's chapter in *Research in Industrial Human Relations,* edited by C. Arensberg et al., Harpers & Brothers, New York, 1957, pp. 131–145.

[2] Fritz J. Rothlisberger and William Dickson, *Management and the Worker,* Harvard University Press, Cambridge, Mass., 1950.

associates. He can only experience the larger organization by indirection, but membership in the small group contributes directly to the shaping of attitudes and behavior toward the entire world of work. For this reason of potency, therefore, the contribution of the small group to the total organization has been a subject of substantial research by those interested in human relations in industry.

Conceptions of the Work Group

As Whyte has pointed out, the individual is not a member of a single group within a larger structure.[3] Rather, the individual interacts in a variety of settings within the organization. It is the task of the researcher to identify those interaction patterns which are focused and concentrated so that it is reasonable to speak of a "group." These he distinguishes from patterns which are sufficiently random so that the elaborations of behavior we associate with the internal life of the small group are not present to any significant degree.

If we follow all the members of the organization through their hours on the job, we are likely to be impressed with this very proliferation of memberships. Most apparent even to the untrained eye is membership, except for that unique individual, the president, in a *subordinate group;* that is, the employee shares a common supervisor with a number of colleagues. Distinguishable from this group, but closely related, is a *functional,* or *task group*—those employees who must collaborate in some fashion if the work task defined by the larger organization is to be accomplished. The boundaries of both of these groups are rather well defined by the larger organization.

However, we see two other kinds of clusterings that tend to overlap and penetrate the organization in unexpected ways. They are not defined by the formal organization and are often included under the general term, informal organization. One of these groups has received a great deal of attention from researchers, the *friendship clique,* whose members are attracted to each other because they gain certain satisfactions from their interactions as such. The other type of group that is less well studied but, we feel, equally important, is the *interest group.* It is comprised of employees who share a common economic interest and who are held together by their desire to gain common objectives within the larger organization.

[3] William F. Whyte, "Small Groups in Large Organizations," *Social Psychology at the Crossroads,* edited by John Rohrer and Muzafer Sherif, Harper & Brothers, New York, 1951, pp. 303–304.

The memberships in these groups are not exclusive; there are many overlappings. Our problem here is to gain some perspective on their interrelations. To do this we shall take a rather close look at some approaches to the study of both the friendship groups or cliques and the task group. From that vantage point we should be able to identify the distinctive characteristics of our interest groups.

THE FRIENDSHIP CLIQUE

This might well be conceived as the elementary building block of human organization. As Mayo writes, "Man's desire to be continuously associated with his fellows is a strong, if not the strongest human characteristic." [4]

At the workplace we thus find an intricate maze of friendship groups representing the diverse interests of the workers who have been placed there by the organization. The exact boundaries of these multiple clusterings appear to reflect the off-the-job interests and associations of the employees, or their previous work experience. As common observation would have it, like-minded individuals are attracted to one another. Age, ethnic background, outside activities, sex, marital status, and so on, comprise the mortar that binds the clique together.

Zaleznik, for example, in his study of a department of relatively unskilled female manual workers, describes this labyrinth of social organization:

> There were mainly female operators on the line, who varied from girls in their late teens to middle-aged women with grown families. Age, and hence common interests, seemed to be one of the dividing lines that marked the organization of informal groups within the line. The older women seemed to group together, while a number of the very young girls who were about to be married or who were contemplating marriage, tended to keep together. Operators #1 and #2 were young men in their late teens or early twenties, and they generally kept apart from the girls on the line. A number of women on the line were divorcees and some of them formed their own little group. Still another social grouping was formed by a few women in their early thirties who had been floaters, or utility operators, in the old plant; these operators were faster workers than the average girl on the line, and they knew more of the work positions on the line as a direct result of their having been floaters in the old plant. Although there seemed to be a clustering of girls in one social group or another, as expressed by their choice of company during the rest periods (two a day lasting ten minutes), the

[4] Elton Mayo, *Social Problems of an Industrial Civilization,* Graduate School of Business Administration, Harvard University, Boston, Mass., 1945, p. 111.

groups tended also to shift somewhat; and a girl could, in some cases, be numbered in, or on the fringe of, several of the informal groups.[5]

From the point of view of the administrator, of what significance are these groups?

An assumption often made concerning these social groups is their universality. Arensberg, in reviewing the Mayo research studies, draws the clearest picture of the indispensable function being served:

> [There] was at hand the notion that the function of social relationships is to bolster the individual, to let him healthily act out his feelings, rather than, sickly, to bottle them up or invert them, to give him motivation, identification and willingness to accept the tight new rationalist controls over work, imposed by taskmasters, now taking the place of older but now dead customary controls. Out of Mayo's watching these worker-to-worker relationships of a new sort unite the lonely, embittered apathetic workers of the mule-spinning room, the doctrine of "informal organization" or "teamwork" seems to have been born.[6]

The friendship group has emerged as the agency which welds the individual to the organization. Loyalty, even attachment, to the total organization with its impersonality, extended hierarchy, and social distance becomes ambiguous. However, attachment to the immediate and easily perceived face-to-face group is the predominant reality of organization experience. For the individual it provides a source of personal security in an impersonal environment. As a result, we are not surprised at the striking results obtained in the study of the American soldier, indicating the importance of the primary group in motivation.[7]

Where cliques are largely nonexistent, as they were in the tumultuous aircraft plants of California which expanded literally overnight into huge aggregations of employees, turnover can be enormous. The presumption is that stable social groups take time to crystallize; during the period of formation many potential members will leave voluntarily because they do not find an established unit with which they can affiliate. This in turn inhibits the formation of permanent groups; the process is self-defeating.

[5] Abraham A. Zaleznik, *Forman Training in a Growing Enterprise,* Graduate School of Business Administration, Harvard University, Boston, Mass., 1951, p. 96.

[6] Conrad Arensberg, "Behavior and Organization," in *Social Psychology at the Crossroads,* edited by John Rohrer and Muzafer Sherif, Harper & Brothers, New York, 1951, p. 339.

[7] Edward Shils, "Primary Groups in the American Army," *Continuities in Social Research,* edited by Robert K. Merton and Paul F. Lazarsfeld, Free Press, Glencoe, Ill., 1950, pp. 16–39.

Lombard and Mayo conclude that the naive administrator who seeks to break up these cliques because of the inefficiency and wasted motion of the purely social activities involved, is actually doing a disservice to the organization.[8] In fact, they find that it takes skillful leadership to encourage their formation, at least in organizations undergoing rapid expansion.

Serious criticism of the universal efficacy of friendship cliques involves consideration of personality differences and work structure differences. A well-known study of "rate busters" and output restricters disclosed a significant minority who were indifferent, if not hostile, to the social groupings they found on the job.[9]

A recent examination of British longshoremen finds that approximately half of the longshoremen on the docks studied have purposely *avoided* the social entanglements of work group membership. Given an opportunity to join semipermanent gangs, they prefer random work assignments that leave them free to come and go at will, with no responsibility.[10] In terms of their personalities, this way is more satisfying to them.

The formation of social groups also appears to be a function of the structure of the work situation itself. Argyris, in a recent study of human relations in a New England bank, finds that the incidence of informal social groupings among tellers is less than for bank employees who do not have that high degree of interaction with customers.[11]

Efforts to find universal solutions to the problems of productivity within the dynamics of the friendship group have not been successful.

Some of the earliest research on productivity was based on the assumption that internal harmony in a work group—reciprocated positive feelings—would produce desirable job performance. Increasingly, however, researchers have become disillusioned with the relationship between social satisfaction and worker effort. Perhaps one of the most telling blows to the impetus to devote substantial energies to building work groups that are sociometrically sound is the provocative study by Goode and Fowler in a low morale plant. They found

[8] Elton Mayo and George F. Lombard, *Teamwork and Labor Turnover in the Aircraft Industry of Southern California,* Graduate School of Business Administration, Harvard University, Boston, Mass., 1940.

[9] Orvis Collins and Donald Roy, "Restriction of Output and Social Clearage in Industry," *Applied Anthropology,* 1946, pp. 1–14.

[10] University of Liverpool, *The Dock Worker,* University Press of Liverpool, Liverpool, England, 1954, pp. 61 ff.

[11] Chris Argyris, *Organization of a Bank,* Yale University, New Haven, Conn., 1954, p. 129.

"the informal relationships which developed were such as to maintain pressures toward high production in the face of considerable *animosity* toward the owners and *among the workers themselves.*"[12] [Italics mine.] Although their findings are severely limited by a unique industrial environment, it has been recognized that the relation between friendship and output cannot be expressed by a simple function.

More recently, Seashore finds in an interesting study in a large heavy equipment manufacturing company that highly cohesive work groups are more likely to have output records that diverge in *either direction* from plant averages.[13] Tightly knit work groups are almost as likely to have notably poor production records as they are likely to have outstandingly good production records. Several years ago a research report on productivity among clerical workers presented what were generally similar findings:

> . . . it was found that there were great differences in the level of production from one friendship group to another . . . the friendship groups had their own groups standards; some to work hard and some to take it easy; some to identify with management and others to aggress against management.[14]

A recent well-received text in the field of public administration comes out strongly on the side of encouraging on-the-job social life to facilitate productivity:

> Although there is some contradictory evidence, the preponderance of evidence indicates that production is actually increased when social conversation is allowed. . . . Restrictions that have the effect of diminishing the pleasantness of the work situation rob the workers of a significant source of satisfaction and can be expected, therefore, to reduce their efforts.[15]

However, a study employing methods of precise interaction observation is unique in casting some doubts as to the positive correlation between social interaction and productivity.

[12] William Goode and Irving Fowler, "Incentive Factors in a Low Morale Plant," *American Sociological Review*, XIV, 1949, p. 624.

[13] Stanley Seashore, *Group Cohesiveness in the Industrial Work Group*, Institute for Social Research, Ann Arbor, Mich., 1954, p. 98.

[14] John R. P. French, Jr. and Alvin Zander, "The Group Dynamics Approach," *Psychology of Labor Management Relations*, edited by Arthur Kornhauser, Industrial Relations Research Association, Champaign Ill., 1949, p. 76.

[15] Herbert Simon, Donald Smithburg, and Victor Thompson, *Public Administration*, Alfred Knopf, New York, 1950, pp. 113–114.

The factory department under discussion seems to show that there is a limit to the supposed relation between an increase in "informal social relations" and an increase in productivity.[16]

Thus the administrator is left with some degree of uncertainty as to the significance of these groupings to his organization.

THE TASK GROUP

In recent years the emphasis in human relations research on work groups has shifted towards greater consideration of the organization of work itself. The layout of the plant and the flow of work provided by the industrial engineer and the placement of supervision controlled by the organizational chart serve to build informal group structures as much as the discovery of common interests and the need for social interaction.

In turn these groups develop norms of behavior and attitude which affect significantly worker effort and loyalty. Most of these center around the interest of the group in controlling: (*a*) the work methods, (*b*) output standards or productivity, and (*c*) relative compensation and prestige relationships. Let us examine each of these in turn.

(*a*) *Impact on Work Methods.* The analogy might be to an electrical current which seeks the path of least resistance. The experience of working in close proximity on a day-to-day basis induces methods that may depart from the organization's original conception of the job, or at least it fills in the specific details of the operation that may not have been specified in the formal work plan. For example, on repetitive jobs employees find it more pleasant to exchange jobs, although such trading is illegal. In the automobile industry, it is a common phenomenon for one worker to do two jobs, while a colleague enjoys an extended rest. Employees change the sequence in which operations are to be performed in order to reduce job tensions and provide short cuts.

Some of these informal, or should we say unplanned for, work methods may decrease worker output. Workers' machinations can overstate make-ready time during job changes. However, other worker innovations undoubtedly increase the total product. One of the most striking cases of the latter was observed by Gross. He found that radar teams through communications circuits set up during so-

[16] A. B. Horsfall and Conrad Arensberg, "Teamwork and Productivity in a Shoe Factory," *Applied Anthropology*, VIII, 1949, p. 13.

cial periods off-the-job were compensating for deficiencies in the information provided by the formal organization. The additional networks provided spontaneously contributed significantly to job success.[17] These informal groups provided interactions which can improve team coordination vastly.

Similarly, researchers have analyzed the initiative exhibited by a group of department store salesmen in evolving a new work pattern that solved a serious internal morale problem, which had been created by a new incentive system. The innovation was so successful both in eliminating interpersonal frictions and in fostering high productivity that top management eventually encouraged its spread to other units of the organization. As the authors conclude: ". . . under further specified conditions the work unit may make and execute decisions ordinarily considered managerial." [18]

However, the formal work structure can be designed so that the elaborations of the informal group necessarily work in opposition to the major objectives of the organization. Recent studies conducted by the Tavistock Institute in England illustrate such organization. One study was designed to examine the effect of changing the method of mining coal:[19]

> The innovation consisted of breaking up the jobs that were previously completed by a small group of miners in one shift into successive operations carried out on a three-shift, 24-hour cycle. As a result, no single group of workers felt responsible for the total operation; work problems that arose on one shift were blamed by the workers on the previous shift. Workers became disinclined to expend additional effort to overcome the natural handicaps that are characteristic of work underground. Local disturbances were magnified by the accumulation of problems as one shift failed to complete a particular task and therefore caused additional hardship for succeeding ones.
>
> On the other hand, in the older method of mining, the total group recognized their responsibility for the operation, since all jobs were done within the group, in one shift. In the older method, individuals whose efforts affected one another came into sufficiently frequent contact to adjust mutually to the work problems that arose. Under the new method such frequency of interaction was impossible; the shifts separated the workers into non-communicating compartments.

[17] Edward Gross, "Some Functional Consequences of Primary Controls in Formal Work Organizations," *American Sociological Review*, XVIII, 1953, pp. 370–371.

[18] Nicholas Babchuck and William Goode, "Work Incentives in a Self-Determined Group," *American Sociological Review*, XVI, 1951, pp. 686.

[19] E. Trist and K. Bamforth, "Some Social and Psychological Consequences of the Long Wall Method of Coal-Getting," *Human Relations*, IV, 1951, pp. 1–38.

Aside from evolving methods which seem most convenient to work group members, the pattern of doing the job is fitted to the status system of the group. Members with most prestige, if at all possible, receive the best jobs. Where possible, working location and equipment are similarly assigned. And where these are not under group control, helping and trading can be adjusted to the status system. The exchange-of-favors system readily responds to the prestige hierarchy.[20] Of course, the evaluation placed on jobs—the differentiation of the more preferred from the less preferred—is itself a product of group interaction.

Whether due to apparent convenience or the exigencies of the status system, the methods evolved within the group for task completion become firmly established. Where outside forces (e.g., technological change) threaten to induce changes, the ranks close and resistance is applied. In part, of course, this may be the natural reaction of the culprit fearing punishment for rule infractions. A more reasonable explanation of the informal group's resistance to change, however, is the intimate relationship between the task group as an entity and the work methods they have evolved. A threat to one is a real threat to the other.

(*b*) *Impact on Output Standards.* Probably more attention has been given to this aspect of task group behavior than to any other. Starting with the work of Mathewson, and extending through the Western Electric studies, we have a long and distinguished line of studies indicating that work groups often formulate quite specific output standards and obtain close conformity from their members in maintaining these standards. Productivity itself is increasingly conceived as a group phenomenon.

There have been several reasons advanced why output control occupies a place of such importance in the life of the group. Work standards are one of the most important aspects of the job which can in some fashion be influenced by worker action. The difficulty of the job, the energy expenditure it requires, is largely determined by the number of units required, rather than by the nature of the job itself. Presumably, without group control management would be able to utilize individual differences and competition for promotion and greater earnings, to establish higher and higher output or performance standards. This would penalize particularly the slower worker and the older employee. It might, however, penalize all

[20] Cf. Ralph Turner, "The Navy Disbursing Officer as a Bureaucrat," *American Sociological Review*, XII, 1947, pp. 342–348.

workers by cutting piece rates where they exist and reducing the number of employees required by the operation. "Run away" output may have internal ramifications. We have observed situations where group controls were weak, and younger, low-prestige employees exceeded the production and earnings records of their betters. The results were calamitous for the internal status hierarchy of the department and ultimately for the effectiveness of the formal organization.[21]

Thus output control is a basic objective of group action as well as an essential element in maintaining group stability. Not only the relation of the members to one another, but the durability of the worker's relation to his job depends on the efficiency of this process. Again we need to note that the resultant is not always unfavorable to management. We have many instances on record where the work group has sanctioned increasingly high productivity.[22]

It should be evident that a great deal of the interest in informal group relations is the product of this presumed relation between output standards evolving within the group and actual worker productivity. There have been many efforts to find the magic formula that would convert low group norms to high group norms.

The evolution of the method of *group decision* for gaining acceptance for changes in production methods and output standards is recognition of the potency of group standards. The theory presumes that leadership methods that involve the entire work group in the change process have two major advantages:

(1) They can eliminate the major barrier of existing group standards which militate against any change, per se.

(2) More positively, they commit the individual to new efforts in the context of his group membership. In a sense, the individual "promises" his fellows to accomplish some change in his behavior. Valuing the opinions of his associates, he feels bound to maintain his agreement.

Ideally, the decision itself becomes the new standard or norm of conduct for the task group. Also, efforts to develop plant-wide incentive systems are premised on the assumption that output and effort are dependent on the relations of the work group to the total social system of the plant.[23]

[21] Leonard R. Sayles, "Impact of Incentives on Inter-Group Work Relations," *Personnel*, XXVIII, 1952, p. 488.

[22] George Strauss, "Group Dynamics and Intergroup Relations," in *Money and Motivation*, William F. Whyte et al., Harper & Brothers, New York, 1955, pp. 90–96.

[23] Cf. William Whyte et al., *Money and Motivation*, *op. cit.*, p. 225.

We find that quality also has a group standard. There are many instances when the management seeks to *reduce* quality, but the workmanship norm resists such changes. This situation is particularly true in skilled groups where management may feel that undue effort is being applied to maintain standards and tolerances that are unnecessary in the light of the eventual use of the product.

(*c*) *Impact on Relative Compensation and Prestige Relations.* The fact that jobs take on a significant social meaning can be seen in the importance attached to wage differentials within the group itself. For example, we have many instances on record where management assigned an equal value to each job and the group found significant distinguishing characteristics. Certain jobs are ranked by employees as *more important or desirable,* and these are expected to have higher earnings than lower ranked jobs. At times, management's own evaluation process will contribute directly to these rankings. The established hierarchy is reinforced, of course, over time, by the gradual perfection of the correlation between the esteem accorded particular workers and the prestige accorded to their jobs. The "more important" workers have moved to the "more important" jobs. (The status of the job is not only a function of the earnings capacity but also the quality of the surroundings, equipment, the tempo of the work required, etc.) Problems occur only when changes are introduced which violate the established hierarchy.[24]

SOME COMMON FEATURES OF THESE GROUPS

Although these several concepts of the informal group are not identical, and in some cases not even complementary in their basic dimensions, they do have one common feature. All emphasize equilibrium: the development of a system of interpersonal relations which stabilizes the work situation (among subordinates and between superior and subordinates), an interconnected series of friendship linkages, work-flow relations, output levels, and status-income relations. The objectives are the maintenance of individual and group stability by insuring a predictability of day-to-day events and effecting a *modus vivendi* between individual on-the-job needs and the requirements of the formal organization.

The clusterings of workers-on-the-job all have these characteristics.

[24] Cf. Leonard R. Sayles, "Worker Values in Job Evaluation," *Personnel,* XXX, 1954; Robert L. Livernash, "Job Evaluation," *Employment and Wages in the United States,* edited by W. S. Woytinsky and associates, Twentieth Century Fund, New York, 1953, pp. 427–435.

The sum of a group of individuals is something more than the total of the constituents; it is a new organization. Because most of the members obtain satisfaction in gaining acceptance as a part of the group, and the group itself wields an influence over its members, there are pressures toward conformity within the group. These pressures result in the establishment of accepted ways of living together. The way of life includes a complex system of customs and rules, vested interests, and interaction patterns which govern the relationship of members of the group to one another and to the larger environment of which it is a part.

The informal group in any and all of its meanings serves well-recognized and accepted human needs. Its existence and continued preservation are hardly matters for surprise. The building up of routines, of established methods of accomplishing tasks, of predictable social relationships, of group roles—these are all elements of structuring which social scientists have found to be typical of the human group. They define the group.

Particularly, through the setting and maintenance of group standards, informal groups have protected their memberships from possible indiscretions that might reflect adversely on them all; also they have provided support for the individual, by acting as a buffer to outside organizations, and by sustaining him through the provision of *known and acceptable* routines of behaving within the face-to-face work group.

Perhaps this whole concept of the stabilizing function of the informal group process is best summarized in the following commentary on the Western Electric researches:

> The Bank Wiring Observation Room seemed to show that action taken in accordance with the technical organization tended to break up, through continual change, the routines and human associations which gave work its value. *The behavior of the employees could be described as an effort to protect themselves against such changes, to give management the least possible opportunity of interfering with them.* When they said that if they increased their output, "something" was likely to happen, a process of this sort was going on in their minds. *But the process was not a conscious one.* It is *important to point out that the protective function of informal organization was not a product of deliberate planning. It was more in the nature of an automatic response . . .*[25] [Italics mine.]

[25] George Homans, "The Western Electric Researches" *Human Factors in Management*, edited by Schuyler Hoslett, Harper & Brothers, New York, 1951, pp, 240–241.

Thus the informal group, as perceived in such studies, *reacts* to the initiations of other organizations, particularly management. Defined in equilibrium terms, the reaction is always an attempt to *preserve* or *regain* the previous undisturbed state—to protect the work methods, social relations, and output levels incorporated in the norms of the group. The goal is always one of security, maintaining the status quo, although, as Homans points out above, the whole protective process is best conceived, not as "deliberate planning" but as an "automatic response" to the industrial system.

Although it has been possible to explain a great deal of in-plant worker behavior in terms of the elaborations induced by informal, face-to-face groups, an element has been lacking. As a result, research studies demonstrate inconsistent or inconclusive findings. The problem appears to center around the concept of the informal group as something apart from the dynamic, collective bargaining environment, and as dependent on immediate, highly personal intragroup relations.

MUTUAL ECONOMIC INTEREST AS THE GROUP FOCUS

We have been describing in all of the previous chapters how the organization of the plant provides incentives for the banding together of individual workers into *interest groups.* These incentives are not only the desire to protect the status quo, work standards, degree of rule enforcement and discipline meted out by supervision, relative earnings, and seniority position, but also include the opportunity to improve their relative position. Improvements can take the form of looser standards, a preferred seniority position, more overtime, more sympathetic supervision, correction of inequities, and better equipment. Many of these benefits often substitute for the more traditional kinds of promotions and mobility.

Although the dictums of personnel administration could lead us to believe that relative wage rates, incentive earnings, promotional ladders, layoff schedules, overtime distribution, quality of working conditions, and work loads are distributed among work groups on the basis of a comprehensive program or system that is independent of pressures, this ideal is rarely attained in practice, if indeed it is an ideal. Work groups do compete among themselves for the available economic rewards.

The distribution of these benefits may be much influenced by the pressures of united and determined informal groups. What management feels is "equitable," just as what the union determines is in the "members' interest," is determined to a large extent by the attitudes expressed by those individuals who can support their demands by group reinforcements. The reality of the in-plant situation offers organized workers many benefits and penalizes relatively, and on occasion absolutely, those work groups which for one reason or another are unable to exercise similar power in the market place of the plant.

At the outset many of these groups may have defensive motives. As Barkin notes in reviewing the organizing history of unions themselves:

> The early efforts of job groups tend to be defensive. They try to keep conditions from getting worse, to protect members of the groups and to prevent destruction of the group itself.[26]

However, it becomes apparent that it is impossible to stand still. Maintaining the same conditions, in a dynamic plant, means sustaining a relative decline in benefits in comparison with those attained by other groups. As in the broader political environment, eternal vigilance is the price of equitable treatment. Even if others were not fighting for increased shares of the economic pie, management is making so many changes in equipment, scheduling, supervision, work methods, and all the rest, that a static position is out of the question.

To repeat, this is not the traditional concept of the informal group seeking conformity with established norms of conduct. These are much more free enterprise units, interacting in a struggle for maximization of utility. This is not to imply that all such groups are equally aggressive in the struggle for self-improvement, or equally well equipped with all the wherewithal to do battle via the union and management grievance procedure and more direct pressure tactics. Some lack the spirit of combat, others the means, whereas only a restricted few are endowed with the characteristics associated with sustained activity and progress toward the goals they seek.

Much of what we say implies a degree of dual or even treble *disloyalty*. Other groups—management, the union, and fellow workers—are perceived as either barriers to or sources of assistance to be manipulated at will.

We were often surprised at the absence of loyalties across group boundaries. Workers showed very little sympathy for the problems

[26] Solomon Barkin, "A Trade Unionist Appraises Management Personnel Philosophy," *Harvard Business Review*, XXXVIII, 1950.

of fellow employees and would even injure the standing of other employees to improve their own conditions.

> For example, in the cushion department of a large automobile body plant, the so-called "pad-up" operation comes before the actual upholstering of the automobile seat. The latter group, called cushion builders, have been traditionally higher skilled and paid, although the wage differential is no longer significant. Nevertheless, they feel themselves very superior to the pad-up men. Management, however, estimates that it takes substantially longer to break in a pad-up man, and his job content requires greater effort. Recently, when models changed and job content was being reapportioned, the cushion builders used their economic strength to shift still additional duties to the pad-up men for which they will not be compensated and which must be performed within the same time period.

From the point of view of the interest group, it is not high identification or loyalty that counts, but rather the right tactics in using or ignoring these other aggregations. Thus, management is neither good nor bad, liked nor disliked as such. In fact, this approach suggests that it may not always be fruitful to think in promanagement and prounion terms. It may well be, as we have suggested, that a group which is satisfied with *itself*, with its ability to protect and improve its own interests, is more favorable to both union and management.

These are interest groups then—the action units which comprise one of the highly dynamic variables within the plant community. The basic distinction is one between groupings that are spontaneous or attributable to the technical requirements of the work process and those which are the conscious result of the self-seeking motives of employees. As an example of the distinction, Chandler notes that there is a distinction between social grouping and the "manner in which the workers aligned themselves in day-to-day collective bargaining activities.[27]

In a sense these are miniature unions:

> Late in the 1920's, a group of skilled workers who sprayed paint on automobile bodies in the plant of a very large manufacturer decided that they could improve their earnings over a period of time by working together as a group. The result was titled "The Sprayer's Club." Without formal recognition from the company, and certainly without any consciousness of being a union, leaders of the Sprayer's Club "negotiated" rates, working conditions, and the number of learners that would be trained with company supervision. For several

[27] Margaret Chandler, *Labor-Management Relations in Illini City, Case Study 3: Garment Manufacture,* University of Illinois, Institute of Labor and Industrial Relations, Champaign, Ill., 1953, p. 456.

years after the plant was formally organized by the UAW-CIO, the Sprayer's Club continued active in furthering the interests of this one group of body sprayers. While formal bargaining authority resided in the union, the club advanced the special interests of this self-conscious group of workmen.

Although the adoption of the club form and a formal name for their group was unique, the association of men sharing common work-created needs is not unusual. In every plant there will be countless numbers of such groups ranging from a short-lived protest movement that attempts to secure higher rates for several men assigned to a newly installed conveyor in a shipping department, to an institutionalized group like the sprayers, who have long-run, continuing problems of mutual concern. Some of these groups begin to hold meetings, either under the aegis of the union, or in spite of it. Some begin to look upon a particular steward as their representative and struggle to elect a man who will defend their interests. A few even adopt written constitutions that define their objectives and their methods of attainment.

Their membership is not limited necessarily to the small face-to-face group. Unlike some of the social groupings described above, their size is not limited by the ability of the individual to respond to others in day-to-day interactions (e.g., inspectors, truckers, substation operators). Whereas so-called primary groups rarely exceed a dozen workmen, concerted interest bodies may contain a hundred or more workers sharing common objectives and acting in concert to further them.

The results for the larger plant may not be a system tending toward equilibrium at all. On the basis of this study we might expect that certain combinations of pressure groups actually involve the organization in increasing instability—a trend toward disequilibrium. We have observed plants where the interaction of these groups involves increasingly greater discontent, turmoil, and non-adaptive behavior; that is, their behavior tends to reinforce the very problems it was designed to solve.

Similarly, the internal structure of these groups is much more responsive to changes in their external environment than is often implied in the concept of the informal work group as a relatively durable, impervious entity. Overnight, technical changes introduced by management can convert a cohesive task force into a disunited rabble, squabbling over internal differences.[28] Similarly, we have

[28] Cf. p. 107.

observed a group of weakly united employees become a force of some magnitude in the social system of the plant within a brief period, with no changes in personnel.[29]

Most important, these interest groups are not static self-preservation societies. Rather they are engaged in the active pursuit of the economic welfare of their membership. Not all of their behavior is intelligently contrived to win the goals they seek, nor are the goals always well-designed or understood, but their basic orientation never changes. Like the union, they want more and more—and still more. The specific goals themselves are not constant, but are continually in flux, as the seniority of the workers in the unit changes as other groups attain or fail to attain certain concessions from management, as the union bargaining platform changes, and as management introduces new equipment and new personnel. In the process these groups contribute much to shaping the industrial relations climate of the plant.

There is no implication that this study has discovered the interest group. On the contrary, many others have preceded us. Two studies are particularly worthy of mention:

In a less well-known section of the now famous Yankee City series the authors make what was at that time a startling observation. In the pre-World War II Newburyport shoe factories, workers' earnings did not correlate very well with the respective skill levels. The authors give a specific example in comparing the earnings of the men in the wood heel departments with those of the makers. Making (or lasting) is a relatively skilled occupation in the shoe factory, compared to the heel department; yet the earnings were substantially higher in the wood heel department. As the authors conclude, "The special explanation for this fact lay in the solidarity of the workers in this department." [30]

Shultz, in a more recent study of the Brockton Shoe industry, observed similar differences in economic strength among various skilled groups (or craft groups) who bargain jointly in the Brotherhood of Shoe Workers. He observes:

> Though these independent unions presumably use their bargaining strength against the employers, they are also the agencies through which

[29] Cf. Leonard R. Sayles, "Intergroup Conflict (The Case of the Grinders)," William F. Whyte et al., *Money and Motivation,* Harper & Brothers, New York, 1955, pp. 67–80.

[30] Lloyd Warner et al., *The Social System of the Modern Factory,* Yale University Press, New Haven, Conn., 1947, p. 186.

Brotherhood members compete for shares in the limited economic welfare available.[31]

He notes in one case that the success of a particular craft group can be attributed to these factors:

> The size, cohesiveness, and work skills of the craft groups vary widely. On the one hand, for example, the highly skilled edge trimmers have organized only one operation, so that a single piece price represents to them a strong, common goal. Each man in the local performs the same work, their total number is 150, and their "share amounts to only about 3 per cent of the total labor cost." [32]

Summary

The emergence of group-sanctioned behavior and attitudes fills out the rationally conceived organization. What on paper is an organization becomes a living, breathing social organism, with all the intricacies, emotions, and contradictions we associate with human relations. Although no organization would long persist which did not provide its members with this opportunity for spontaneous human relations, a major problem of the larger organization becomes one of successfully incorporating these groupings.

We have found that it is inappropriate to speak of the informal group. Rather we suggest that it is more useful to investigate the relationship among friendship cliques, work teams and pressure or interest groups. Not only is there obviously substantial overlapping in group membership, but the internal structure of any one of them is shaped by the membership it includes, as well as by the membership it excludes. Thus, as we have seen, the concerted interest force exerted by a pressure group is reduced by the extent to which technology complicates work team relations and separates tightly knit and exclusive friendship cliques. The impact can flow in the opposite direction as well. Unsuccessful interest group activity, the inability to defend the entire group's economic welfare, leads to interpersonal squabbles and recriminations that vitiate social satisfactions on the job.

Our whole emphasis has involved a shift from concentrating on the informal group to the relation of work group behavior to the technological and organizational setting. Thus we have moved from the

[31] George P. Shultz, *Pressures on Wage Decisions*, John Wiley and Sons, New York, 1951, p. 103.

[32] *Ibid.*

individual case study in an individual plant to comparative studies of groups in a variety of formal organizations. Our objective has been to understand better the diversity of employee reactions to management and the union as they manifest themselves in the setting of the work group.

Recently there has been criticism of human relations research for its failure to study informal groups in the setting of the larger formal organizational structure. It is argued that there has been an overemphasis on interpersonal and even intragroup relations as isolated phenomenon apart from their dependence on the total environment.

> . . . the emphasis is all on human relations, but these relationships appear to be isolated atoms somewhat suspended in free space. Specifically, human relations are generally treated as if they were attributes of individuals, and the group structures of which they are component parts as well as the larger organization of which these groups are parts are neglected in the analysis.[33]
>
> (The work of Mayo) . . . led us, for a time, to neglect the machine and the content of the job and to swing entirely over to a consideration of the pattern of relations among men. We seemed to be assuming that technology and the job were unimportant, and that the controlling factors in worker satisfaction and in work group behavior were found in the relations among workers and management people.[34]

In small measure we hope this study has suggested one approach to answering these challenges.

[33] Peter Blau, "Formal Organization: Dimensions of Analysis," paper prepared for the fifty-first annual meeting of the American Sociological Society, Detroit, Mich., September 7–9, 1956.

[34] William F. Whyte, "On the Evolution of Industrial Sociology," paper prepared for the fifty-first annual meeting of the American Sociological Society, Detroit, Mich., September 7–9, 1956.

chapter 7

Summary: technology, work structure, and group behavior

This study was designed to explore a very elementary unit in the structure of industrial relations, the work group. It focused on the behavior of work groups and particularly on concerted behavior actuated by the self-interest of the members. Our objective was to explain differences in behavior among work groups. We wished to discover whether certain aspects of employee day-to-day behavior could be related to the *structure of the work group*, as determined by the technology of the enterprise, independent of supervisory skills (or their absence), management and union pressures, and individual personality variables.

At the level of everyday observation we find that each plant has certain departments that are more troublesome or more cooperative than the average. The incidence of serious breaches of plant discipline such as wildcat strikes and the occurrence of formal and informal grievances are not randomly distributed. Some related studies have shown that participation in intraunion activities is also concentrated in a relatively small proportion of the total plant population. Both managers and union officers often take into account the existence and the influence of these informal clusters of workers (although often without conscious attention to the important role they are playing).

Our basic theme has been: although at any one time particular work groups may tend to be more (or less) management or union oriented, such attitudes are less important in explaining the industrial relations life of the plant, than the *dynamic relationships among concerted interest aggregations.* At a particular period some of these groups may be in relative equilibrium, but many are motivated to

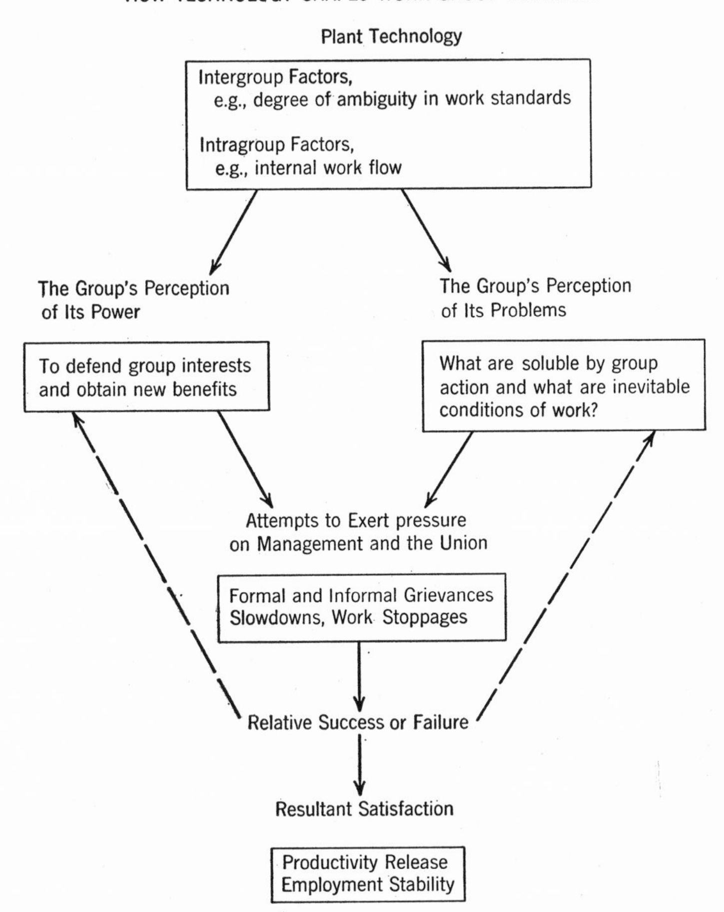

The above illustrates diagrammatically the relation of plant technology to work group behavior. Technology directly affects the group's perception of both the work problems it believes are soluble by concerted effort and the relative power it can muster to do battle for these. In turn, these two factors are responsible for the number and quality of pressure tactics utilized against management and the union. The success or failure of these efforts to originate changes in benefits enjoyed contributes to employment stability and productivity. These experiences also feed back information shaping group judgment on whether future forays for similar objectives are worth future sacrifices.

gain new benefits or defend old ones. Their efforts in such endeavors will be instrumental in shaping the effectiveness of management and union policies.

We also hoped to add in some small measure to the understanding of plant-level industrial relations. We believe that a relatively small number of work groups within an industrial plant play a vital role in determining the climate and events that shape its industrial relations character. The behavior of the groups and its sources are, we believe, predictable. Further, the total manufacturing process sets very real limits to the effectiveness of certain patterns of supervision and union-management relationships.

To many it may have appeared naive, even misleading, to discuss grievance behavior, as often as we have, without more explicit reference to the nature of the issues involved, and the positions of the parties to the dispute. Surely, it will be argued, grievances, slowdowns, strikes, all must be related to what employees, managers, and union leaders struggle over within the plant. This fact can hardly be denied. But what has appeared of equal significance is that the *quantity* of dissatisfaction expressed and its *quality* (the methods utilized by employees in attempting to solve a work-oriented problem) were relatable to specific organizational variables. What one group saw as a problem, another group might be willing to accept as an inevitable condition of work. The attitudes of employees were a product of the structural conditions of work.

This type of analysis has also involved a concept of the grievance procedure in industry which is broader than the rather legalistic definitions incorporated in union-management contracts. Employee protests, complaints, grievances, and pressure tactics, are all efforts to communicate upward in the organization, to initiate change. This is in contrast to the more usual position they fill in the organization: responding to the orders and initiations of both management and union representatives. In such a process it is impossible to separate the true grievances (charges the contract has been violated) from the efforts at negotiating (or bargaining) more advantageous conditions of work, or from aggressive demonstrations of accumulated frustrations. Organizationally these grievances are indistinguishable in that employees, not those above them in the hierarchy, are originating the activity.[1]

Such data would hardly be meaningful unless it could be shown

[1] Professor James Kuhn of Columbia is engaged in a challenging inquiry which seeks to explore the many ramifications of the grievance procedure in industry. My thinking here has benefited from his analysis.

that we can predict *which* departments or work groups in a particular plant will exhibit these kinds of behavior, without knowing the specific composition of the group, the qualities of the supervisor, or the state of union-management relations. We can, in fact, make such judgments with a fair degree of accuracy. In a given plant certain work groups will consistently exhibit characteristic behavior even though their supervisor is changed (for better or for worse) and union-management relations mature or deteriorate. We very often find that certain occupational groups are known throughout an industry for their highly characteristic behavior. These similarities of behavior, associated with a given kind or type of work group, are the subject of our research.[2]

SIGNIFICANCE OF OCCUPATION

At one level, this is a study of the significance of occupation, of type of work, for the demonstrated behavior of job incumbents. Although the study concentrates on a relatively narrow group of "blue-collar" jobs, it is hoped that some of the same techniques, and some of the same variables as well will be applicable to a much wider range of occupations.

A substantial amount of research in the social sciences has indicated that the worker is occupationally oriented; men are bound together by shared work experiences and attitudes. We usually think of "occupation" as referring to the well-defined professions and crafts as well as the "would be" professions and trades. Employees in the modern factory, with its emphasis on machine output, with the exception of a small number of traditional craftsmen required to construct and maintain the physical facilities, fit into no well defined occupational pattern, except the very broad one of "semiskilled factory worker." Except for membership in this amorphous classification, industrial workers are not thought to have other occupational ties. A close examination of the day-to-day functioning of the plant, however, belies this assumption. Workers do, in fact, behave as though they belonged to highly specific occupational groups. We have

[2] In a very interesting study of a huge housing project near Chicago, Park Forest, William H. Whyte Jr., of the *Fortune* editorial staff noted that certain courts (blocks within the subdivision in which apartments faced one another across a common grass area) always produced neighborhood leaders whereas others rarely did. Similarly, some courts were consistent trouble spots and sources of complaints while others were quite the opposite. These differences in behavior patterns persisted even though the residents changed frequently! *Fortune*, July 1953, Vol. 48, p. 88.

sought to explore the basis for this identification and its impact on the plant and more particularly the kinds of differences that develop among plant occupations.

The following, taken from a quite different context, summarizes some of our own conclusions:

> The collective agreement applies to the relationship of a large number of people of various personalities, temperaments, ambitions, fears, and tensions. While we speak of "the employer" and "the union" as entities, the agreement deals not merely with the relationship of these two institutions, but even more with the relations between numerous people—machine hands, laborers, craftsmen, rate checkers, plant policemen, several ranks of foremen, labor relations men, superintendents, and so on. To think merely in terms of "employer" and "employee" or "management" and "union" is to miss a very important fact in labor relations—the fact that the relationship involves numerous people whose interests, needs, jobs and performances cannot be compressed without distortion into two general rubrics.[3]

SIGNIFICANCE OF TECHNOLOGY

More specifically, this report should have some significance for the industrial engineer, the student of organization and work flow, and the manager who is concerned with the relationship between the manufacturing process and human relations. In another context the author has expressed his view that engineering variables and personnel variables are not unrelated, and that the "human relations approach" involves an understanding of the relation of technology to the functioning of the organization.[4]

Ideally, it should be possible to develop predictive tools that would permit the design of organizations for specific personnel or industrial relations characteristics. The millennium is nowhere in sight, we quickly add, but our research should move us in this direction. A society characterized by a dynamic technology can ill afford to ignore the relation of this technology to the reactions of the work force recruited to man the machines and factories.

For almost exactly the same reasons the union leader, whether designing an organizational campaign or servicing an existing local, needs much more information concerning the reactions of various kinds of work groups to the union, and its internal life, to incentive

[3] Harry Shulman and Neil W. Chamberlain, *Cases on Labor Relations*, The Foundation Press, Brooklyn, N. Y., 1949, p. 4.

[4] Leonard Sayles, "Human Relations and the Organization of Work," *Michigan Business Review*, VI, 1954, pp. 21–25.

plans, job classification, seniority and all the rest, and most specifically to the grievance procedure.

Both management and the union reserve such epithets as "prima donnas," "troublemakers," and "hot heads" for groups whose motives and behavior in the plant community leave something to be desired. Although they prefer to believe radical leadership is the cause, this hypothesis is quickly destroyed. We have seen, for example, Strategic or Erratic behavior patterns are perpetuated over long periods, although the offending leaders may have been removed, and the objects of the aggression eliminated.

However, we did observe certain groups which were more susceptible to the personalities of strong leaders. We concluded that Apathetic and Erratic groups sought out and responded positively to charismatic leaders. Thus, if they were subject to the influence of a highly aggressive individual, with the ability to attract a following, they might develop more hostile relations with management or the union than if no such member was included within their group. At the same time they were also subject to rapid conversions to good relations through some newly acquired leader.

We also sought to explain overall differences among the industrial relations climates of some of the plants in the study. Plants where most operations were technologically interdependent were likely to be highly cooperative or highly antagonistic in their union-management relations. Those with a number of insulated, self-sufficient departments (and where some at least were characterized by individual operations) could not easily fall into either of these extreme relationships, because the union officers were kept occupied responding to the insistent self-interest demands of these work groups. Relations in these plants were in the middle ranges, neither outstandingly good nor bad.

WHAT IS HUMAN RELATIONS RESEARCH?

One further value of this kind of research may be to highlight some misconceptions concerning the nature of human relations research. Many critics see the developing field of human relations as emphasizing solely interpersonal *communications* variables. The typical problem they believe is dealt with here is lack of common understanding due to individual ineptness, or personality difficulties. The critics believe the findings of human relations research could be summarized as follows: "If you can somehow cause people to 'see the other fellow's point of view,' any conflict of interest between them will disappear." The causal factors, these critics feel, are always personal, individual shortcomings.[5]

Given this conception, perhaps overstated, it is no wonder that observers who recognize the influence of environmental and historical forces in human relations are hostile or, at best, amused at the naïveté that would place such heavy weight on face-to-face relations or group dynamics.

In fact, many researchers who are blanketed-in under the reproachful term "human relations" deal directly and specifically with environmental forces, particularly structural forces. One conclusion of the present study is that broad technological factors play a significant role in determining the characteristics of work group behavior.

To be sure, some researchers, as well as management, have tended to put human relations and problems relating to the organization of work in separate, watertight compartments.[6] Under these assumptions the researcher is either interested in the skills of dealing with the human element at work (human relations) or the engineering problem of efficient organizational design. Although it is possible to change the pattern of human relations in the organization without changing the technology, the arrangement of jobs, and the organizational structure, the reverse is probably not true.

INFORMAL GROUPS AS A MEANS OF PARTICIPATION

On the subject of worker participation in plant decisions affecting their livelihood and satisfactions, we tend to restrict our thinking to two rather distinct levels. On the one hand, we have the development of research and practice on methods by which the supervisor can effectively utilize the subordinate group to complement his own leadership and decision-making ability (participative management). This has the two advantages of more economical use of employee ideas and knowledge, and greater likelihood that worker support will be given to decisions finally made. On the other hand, the literature of union-management relations stresses the role of unions in giving the worker an opportunity to participate in industrial management.

It is our belief, however, that individual workers are probably most

[5] Cf. Clark Kerr and Abraham Siegel, "The Interindustry Propensity to Strike—An International Comparison," *Industrial Conflict*, edited by A. Kornhauser, R. Dubin and A. Ross, McGraw-Hill Book Co., New York, 1954, p. 199.

[6] Cf. William F. Whyte, "Human Relations Theory—A Progress Report," *Harvard Business Review*, XXXIV, No. 5, 1956, p. 132.

successful in influencing both the decisions of their supervisors and the policies and programs of their local unions when they act in concert—through the medium of their own work groups. It is at this *intermediate level* (between the individual and the union), perhaps more than at any other, that worker points of view and interests can be effective in influencing the thinking of the union leadership and the company management. The local union is an organization which cannot automatically serve the multifarious and often conflicting needs of members who owe allegiance to it. Few political organizations, in fact, will be responsive to a rabble of individuals.

Insofar as common interests are represented in the informal group, their expression will be amplified many times beyond the single voice in the department meeting or individual grievance in the union files.

On a more theoretical level there is no reason why we should distinguish between the interactions involved in the more traditional superior-subordinate decision-making process and those relevant to the redress procedures embodied in the collective bargaining agreement. In terms of the social system of the factory, there is no difference. Both can involve participation, or *upward initiation*, as we would define the concept.

Management is often told that it must learn to work with "groups" since employees, under many circumstances, do not respond as individuals to company action. In fact, it is becoming almost commonplace to speak of the supervisor's responsibility for learning to deal effectively with his subordinates as an informal group, with its unique leadership, beliefs, and customs. Research in recent years has given rise to a whole new conception of leadership that involves the utilization of group methods: conferences, group decision, and representative shop government.

In all of the discussions of working with the informal group, there is a tacit assumption that basically all groups are alike, and the only unique feature with which the supervisor need acquaint himself is the fact that a group is something other than the sum of the individuals included, that there is a plus factor which makes the whole something more than the sum of its parts. A good deal of effort therefore goes into teaching supervisors what a group "is."

In a sense, in this report we are challenging the previous assertion. We are suggesting that there are highly significant differences among work groups, and before the supervisor (or the union organizer or officer as well) can deal effectively with the work group, he needs to know much more about these differences. Often we have tended mistakenly to place full responsibility on the supervisor for his group's behavior: Employee-centered supervisors are supposed to build prideful work groups that are likely to demonstrate high productivity. While the supervisor's behavior is certainly not without effect, our data would indicate that there are many facets of group behavior which can more readily be related to the internal structure of the group and its relative position in the total plant structure than to the behavior of the supervisor. Hence, a work group is not one pattern of employee responses, but rather a whole range of possible behavior.

We have suggested that to explain this range of group behavior we need to relate the work structure (as determined by technology) and the associated social structure to their potential for economic interest groupings. Realistically, we can no longer ignore the fact that workers in unionized plants attempt to protect and improve what they feel is important about their jobs through group action, and these groups cannot be separated from work and social aggregations. The complexity of our discussion has been primarily due to this attempt to explain the dynamic relation between work teams (technological units), friendship cliques, and pressure groups (economic units). We have attempted to suggest possible interrelations between these kinds of groups, the power they exert, the satisfaction they provide their members, and the level of productivity they motivate.

Thus, the informal work group is something more than an unplanned-for modification of the formal organization that influences workers' attitudes and ties them together in meaningful social wholes. It is also a dynamic factor in shaping the critical pressures and decisions which are partially responsible for the industrial relations climate of the plant. In some instances these interest groupings can move the plant toward *disequilibrium* rather than toward the snug harmony and balance envisioned by Mayo and his followers.

CONCLUSION

We have endeavored to determine the circumstances, the types of leadership, and the membership characteristics which enable certain interest groups within the plant to determine and express their wants, to solve their problems, and to accommodate to technical and economic requirements, as well as to the union while others fail in the process. Concentrating on the environmental characteristics associated with certain typical behavior patterns, we have been able to explain in part why some groups are noted for internal bickerings, festering grievances or blowups, and why others are renowned for their self-control, unity, and ability to adapt to new circumstances.

Managers and union leaders are under almost constant pressure from employees to bring about certain adjustments. This study has dealt with some of the origins of these rank-and-file pressures and their role in the organization. Additional knowledge of this sub-level of the union-management relationships may assist both parties to promote stable and mutually satisfying collective bargaining. It should also contribute to the abilities of the personnel administrator and student of human relations who seek to understand the functioning of the industrial plant.

Appendix: research method

It should be re-emphasized that our largest source of data for this study was the descriptions provided for us by management (primarily) and union officials of differences in the industrial relations behavior of various parts of their respective plants over a period of time and of the technology of the plants themselves. Because of the nature of the information requested and the minimum threat involved to the status or reputation of the informant, we believed that this was a satisfactory, although highly imperfect research method.

At the level of the first-line supervisor there was a problem with the interviewee being concerned with how he was "showing up" in the interview. Within management itself and sometimes between management and union there might be differences in the evaluation of particular work groups, whether from their respective points of view these were good or bad groups (although we were surprised at the preponderance of agreement in this area), but there did not seem to be significant differences in their descriptions of the *behavior* of these groups. Since the study was conducted entirely by one person, the author, and there was a need for a relatively large sample of groups, other techniques did not appear feasible.

The author has leaned heavily, perhaps too heavily, on knowledge acquired in other research projects to help explain and interpret the attitudes and behavior exhibited. Much of the basic framework for the study evolved from the research conducted by Dr. George Strauss and the author that is incorporated in *The Local Union.*

We did not begin as though we were looking at the industrial relations of an organization at the work group level for the first time. Admittedly, then, we began our study with certain strong assumptions. Essentially these involved the important role played by groups of like-minded employees, sharing some occupational identification, in the day-to-day functioning of the grievance procedure. We felt that the system of industrial jurisprudence created by unionization or other institutionalized appeal procedures weighed heavily in favor of the group, as compared to the individual or the totality of employees.

In each plant we followed roughly the same technique, although there were variations depending on the ease of entry and acceptance for the study. We interviewed a sample of the top level of the plant management first, ideally, both line and staff. We toured the operations, observing the relative location of work areas, the work operations, and the technology employed. This was supplemented by verbal descriptions of work methods and work flow in the organization. We then requested permission to interview departmental supervisors and/or union officials. Interviews with union officials were refused us by management in about half our cases. From our discussions we tried to crystallize a picture of the divisions within the plant, whether supervisory, trade, machine group, unit, department, work crew, assembly line, or shift, that were consistently mentioned as acting concertedly. Thus in our earlier interviews within any organization our questions about "groups" were left purposely vague to obtain from the informants themselves perceptions of what were the significant clusters of employees for self-interest activities. Our questions became more specific, relating to particular groups, after we had spent some time in the organization. This was a type of "progressive interviewing." As we gained additional information, we probed more deeply into certain work areas and problems.

Following is a list of the areas explored through our interviewing. The exact phrasing of the questions varied according to: whether management or union was being interviewed, the informant's level in the organization, and the amount of information obtained from others that was available for cross-checking. In every case we tried to obtain information on the length of time the particular characteristic had been relevant to the group in question.

We also encouraged our informants to review for us grievance records, production and quality records, requests for transfers, bids for posted jobs, and other data which would help us evaluate the impact of the informal groups in each plant.

1. *History of the Plant*
    A. What are the most important jobs in the plant? The most important skills? The least important?
    B. Which are the key jobs as far as keeping the plant operating is concerned? Which are the most profitable operations? The least profitable?
    C. Has this changed very much? Were different groups in these positions in the past? What about the future?
    D. What have been the major problems in the plant, grievances, requests for change, etc? Affecting whom?
2. *Group Relationships to Management*
    A. Which group would you take most seriously if it threatened to walk out or to slow down because one of its grievances was not satisfied? Which would you take least seriously?
    B. Which do you feel are the most cooperative groups in the plant; the most responsible and consistent—which the least so?
    C. Which groups do you think are most influential? The most active in pressing their demands?—that others respect the most?
    D. Which groups are the most productive, cooperative, loyal? Which are the least so?
    E. Where do most of the grievances come from? What were they? How were they handled? Which are consistently appealed over the head of the superior? Which not?
    F. What did _____ group do when _____ happened? (Based on answers to previous questions)
    G. Which groups most readily follow instructions? Where do you have the most serious problems finding adequate supervision? When is there considerable turnover in supervision?
    H. Formality of relations with supervisor versus informality.
    I. Which can handle their own problems best?
3. *Personnel Administration Area*
    A. Where is turnover and absenteeism highest in the plant? Where the lowest?
    B. Which are the most popular jobs, the least popular jobs?
    C. Which groups are doing best as far as meeting production standards? Which worst?
    D. Where in the plant have you made changes recently in wages, hours, working conditions, etc.? Why were these changes made?
4. *Internal Group Relations*
    A. Which would you say are the most tightly knit groups?
    B. Which groups are rather informal in their work relations, exchange work with one another and reassign tasks for one another, etc.?
    C. Identification of formal, informal and functional leaders. Is the steward the real leader?
    D. Evaluation of these leaders; type of person chosen as a leader—his personality.

E. Which groups seem to have internal difficulties—e.g., members squabbling with one another (tension incidents)?

5. *Technology of Particular Groups*
   A. Position in the flow of work.
   B. Predictability of the work versus variability of materials and working conditions.
   C. How much control does the supervisor have to exercise?
   D. Technologically determined interactions among group members.
   E. How easily can exact rank and standards be defined for the group?
6. *Intergroup Relations*
   A. Any key or base groups (to which others compare themselves)?
   B. Which envied? Which most powerful, etc.?
   C. Who supports whom?
   D. Reputation for best conditions? Worst conditions?
   E. Which most united? Least united?
7. *Relations with the Union*
   A. Active, not active; pro- or anti-union? Changes over time.
   B. Grievances filed and those raised informally.
   C. Measures of success in this regard (concessions in contract, voluntary changes).
   D. Attendance at union meetings.
   E. Voting behavior—solidly behind certain candidate versus split votes in the area.
   F. Number of candidates for top union office from this group: successful and unsuccessful.
   G. Stewards and bargaining committee candidates.
      1. Number of candidates in the past.
      2. Job status of the candidates.

We have included a summary interview schedule for departments where we were able to talk with hourly employees. Our questions varied depending on the amount of information we had previously obtained from other sources. However, the questions were all directed to grievances or problems the group had expressed in some fashion to management or the union, the attitudes toward these problems, their source, predictions as to their solution, and general attitudes toward relations with management and the union.

Below is a general outline of the approach which was taken in each rank-and-file interview.

1. Introduction; what kind of job was this? What was good about it (in comparison to other jobs that they know of in the plant)? What was bad about it (again in comparison to other jobs)? To what extent did one man's work depend on the work of another? That is, if it was an assembly line, to what extent did the pace at which other people perform control how fast or how slow he worked! To what extent were his efforts independent of or dependent on the efforts of others?
2. The major problems the man in his work group faced were: How

has the job changed over time? Was it at one time a better or a worse job? How did the future look? More specifically, what happened in terms of particular problems workers have experienced? What were the problems and how were they handled? For example, did the group use the grievance procedure, a slowdown, an actual work stoppage, informal pressures on the supervisor or on other union officials, etc.?

How important was the informal leader? Did the department regularly elect a union representative who represented them on the union committee? What were the various steps that the group took in a particular problem? What did they do first? What second, etc., until the final conclusion, and how did they feel about the final result?

3. What was the relationship between this work group and other work groups? How much support did they get from other departments or work groups, and in turn how much support or help had they given others in winning their grievances and demands?

4. How well did the men get along with each other? Were there ever fights in the group? How tightly knit a work group was this?

5. The informant was asked to compare his present work group with other groups that he knows about or thinks he knows about. This was an attempt to get some scaling of the relatively most successful work departments as far as getting their grievances won. Which was the least successful? Which were the most united groups that stuck together when they had a problem? Which the least united? For example, "How does your work group compare with these others?" Which groups were most influential in having some effect on union policy? Which were most influential in having an impact on management? Which groups were taken most seriously if they threatened a grievance or a slowdown or a strike by management or the union?

The major portion of the field work for this study was undertaken within the state of Michigan during the period 1954–56. Where adequate information was available, studies completed earlier for research on *The Local Union* were combined with the more recently collected data. However, these comprised less than 10 per cent of the total.

Our data is derived from research conducted in twenty-two plants, where we were given access for relatively intensive work, and eight other companies in which less systematic inquiry was possible. The industry sampling is biased greatly in favor of metal processing, both in the capital goods and consumer fields. Approximately one-third of the sample is comprised of firms associated with the automobile industry, either in terms of parts manufacture or production of the vehicle itself. Others sampled include basic steel and fabricated steel, bearings, diesel motors, office equipment, photographic equipment, boilers and radiators, home appliances, and electric motors.

Outside the metalworking field we were able to study companies manufacturing wood furniture, fiber cartons, breakfast foods, chemicals, and those engaged in the production and distribution of power.

Included in the data are six intensive department studies ranging in size from thirty to sixty employees. In each of these we were able to interview a minimum of 25 per cent of the total group.

The total comprises data on approximately 300 work groups. However, it would be misleading to suggest that each was complete in terms of the questions listed above. Because we worked without assistance and sought to obtain rather extensive coverage, we were unable to assure ourselves we had comparable information in each case. There were frequently serious gaps in the data as well as suggested findings that could not be cross-checked. For these reasons it seemed inappropriate and equally misleading to attempt systematic quantification and the use of correlation techniques. Although statistics could be applied here, they would give more the impression of validity.

As a result, the findings cited are the product of testing a series of alternative hypotheses by inspection of the data. Work group characteristics, including job descriptions and behavior with respect to management, the union, and the grievance procedure, were arrayed in large tables. The general scheme which appeared to provide a reasonably close fit has been described in this volume.

At the present time, through the interest and skill of Dr. William Schwarzbek, of the staff of the General Electric Company's Public and Employee Relations Research group, most of the hypotheses presented here are being tested by more precise quantitative tools.

In conclusion we should like to add that at this stage of our knowledge it seemed to the author, rightly or wrongly, that the present pattern analysis, suggesting the *direction* of variation, was more useful than precise quantification that could only encompass a substantially smaller range of variables.

Index